MW00973802

CON 127
Contract Management

Second Edition

Note to Students:

Changes in public laws and regulations pertaining to federal contracting occur regularly. If portions of this textbook have been affected by recent changes, you may ask your instructor to update them orally as needed.

Portions of this document include Government generated public domain materials from the Federal Acquisition Regulatory Council, the Department of Defense, and Defense Acquisition University.

ISBN-13: 978-1987529104
ISBN-10: 1987529103

This Page Intentionally Left Blank

Table of Contents

This Page Intentionally Left Blank

This Page Intentionally Left Blank

Chapter 1 - Administrative Roles and Responsibilit

Introduction

Contract Administration involves those activities performed by Government officials after a contract has been awarded to determine how well the Government and the contractor performed to meet the requirements of the contract. It encompasses all dealings between the Government and the contractor from the time the contract is awarded until the work has been completed and accepted or the contract terminated, payment has been made, and disputes have been resolved. As such, contract administration constitutes that primary part of the procurement process that assures the Government gets what it paid for.

In contract administration, the focus is on obtaining supplies and services, of the requisite quality, on time, and within budget. While the legal requirements of the contract are determinative of the proper course of action of Government officials in administering a contract, the exercise of skill and judgment is often required in order to protect the public interest effectively.

The specific nature and extent of contract administration vary from contract to contract. It can range from the minimum acceptance of a deliverable and payment to the contractor to extensive involvement by program, audit, and procurement officials throughout the contract term. Factors influencing the degree of contract administration include the nature of the work, the type of contract, and the experience and commitment of the personnel involved. Contract administration starts with developing clear, concise performance-based statements of work to the extent possible, and preparing a contract administration plan that cost-effectively measures the contractor's performance and provides documentation to pay accordingly.

Effective communication between the Government and the contractor helps to achieve a clear and mutual understanding of the contract requirements. Contractors need to understand the roles and responsibilities of the Government officials who will administer the contract. Government contracting officials must clearly understand their specific responsibilities and restrictions in administering the contract. Those concerns include such things as the authority of Government personnel who will administer the contract, quality control and testing, the specific contract deliverable requirements, special contract provisions, the government's procedures for monitoring and measuring performance, contractor billing, voucher approval, and payment procedures.

Contract administration requires the interaction of the Contracting Officer and the contractor. The Procuring Contracting Officer (PCO) can delegate certain contract administration functions to the Administrative Contracting Officer (ACO).

Primary Players

The Procurement Contracting Officer (PCO) is the individual who negotiates and awards contracts and resolves most day-to-day contracting matters. The Administrative Contracting Officer (ACO) is assigned after contract award.

The table below provides examples of different responsibilities.

PCO	ACO	Contractor
• Receives specifications for inspection, testing, etc. from the program manager/ customer. • Ascertains appropriate requirements for the contractor's quality control are included in solicitations and contracts. • Issues necessary instructions to the cognizant Contract Administration Office. • Verifies contractor fulfillment of contract quality requirements. • Ensures non-conformances are identified.	• Develops and applies quality assurance procedures. • Verifies whether or not supplies/ services conform to contract requirements. • Maintains records reflecting quality assurance actions. • Implements any specific written instructions from the Contracting Officer. • Reports any defects observed in design or technical requirements. • Recommends changes necessary to provide more effective operations.	• Controls the quality of supplies and/or services. • Provides only those supplies/ services that conform to contract requirements. • Ensures that vendors/suppliers have an acceptable quality control system. • Performs all inspections and test required by the contract.

FAR Definitions

The following key terms are important to contract administration.

FAR 46.101 and 2.101 provide the following key definitions:

Acceptance: The act of an authorized representative of the Government by which the Government assumes ownership of existing identified supplies or approves specific services rendered as the partial or complete performance of a contract.

Commercial-Off-The-Shelf (COTS) item: An item produced and placed in stock by a contractor, or stocked by a distributor, before receiving orders or contracts for its sale.

Conditional acceptance: Acceptance of supplies or services that do not conform to contract quality requirements, or are otherwise incomplete, that the contractor is required to correct or otherwise complete by a specified date.

Contract quality requirements: The technical requirements in the contract relating to the quality of the product or service and those contract clauses prescribing inspection, and other quality controls incumbent on the contractor, to assure that the product or service conforms to the contractual requirements.

Government contract quality assurance: The various functions, including inspection, performed by the Government to determine whether a contractor has fulfilled the contract obligations pertaining to quality and quantity.

Patent defect: Any defect which exists at the time of acceptance and is not a latent defect.

Major nonconformance: Means a nonconformance, other than critical, that is likely to result in failure of the supplies or services, or to materially reduce the usability of the supplies or services for their intended purpose.

Minor nonconformance: Means a nonconformance that is not likely to materially reduce the usability of the supplies or services for their intended purpose, or is a departure from established standards having little bearing on the effective use or operation of the supplies or services.

Inspection: Examining and testing supplies or services to determine whether they conform to contract requirements.

Performance Monitoring Terms

Under a contract, both parties are obligated to perform in accordance with the terms and conditions as stated in the contract. Not all contracts, however, are performed according to their terms and conditions or within required time frames. Poor performance or late deliveries may cause costly delays to the Government. Thus, the Government monitors contract performance to ensure that the required supplies or services are delivered on time.

Performance monitoring involves contract administration activities that Contracting Officers and other Government personnel use to ensure that supplies or services acquired under contracts conform to prescribed quality, quantity, and other requirements called out in the contract and its clauses.

Government Policy on Performance Monitoring

As stated in FAR 46.102, it is a Government-wide policy that requires agencies to ensure that deliverables provided by contractors meet contract requirements and that procedures are in place for assuring contract requirements are met before the acceptance of deliverables. Also, no contract precludes the Government from performing appropriate inspection and acceptance measures and from using another agency's inspection and acceptance services when it is more practical or beneficial to the Government.

Contracts for commercial items rely on the contractor's existing quality assurance system. This is done as a substitute for compliance with Government inspection and testing unless it is a customary market practice that permits a buyer's in-process inspection, as stated in FAR 46.102. Performance must be monitored and documented. However, even in commercial contracts, the Government never waives its rights to conduct an inspection. Any in-process inspection by the Government shall be conducted in a manner consistent with commercial practice.

FAR 46.102 states agencies shall ensure that:

(a) Contracts include inspection and other quality requirements, including warranty clauses when appropriate, that are determined necessary to protect the Government's interest.

(b) Supplies or services tendered by contractors meet contract requirements;

(c) Government contract quality assurance is conducted before acceptance (except as otherwise provided in this part), by or under the direction of Government personnel;

(d) No contract precludes the Government from performing inspection;

(e) Nonconforming supplies or services are rejected, except as otherwise provided in 46.407;

(f) Contracts for commercial items shall rely on a contractor's existing quality assurance system as a substitute for compliance with Government inspection and testing before tender for acceptance unless customary market practices for the commercial item being acquired permit in-process inspection (Section 8002 of Public Law 103-355). Any in-process inspection by the Government shall be conducted in a manner consistent with commercial practice; and

(g) The quality assurance and acceptance services of other agencies are used when this will be effective, economical, or otherwise in the Government's interest (see Subpart 42.1.)

Monitoring Requirements

Performance monitoring not only considers the contractor's performance but it also ensures that Government technical and other support personnel do not authorize the contractor to perform unintended changes to the contract that generally result from either a specific action or a failure to act.

Communication is very important, and the key to effective contract administration. All Government officials involved in contract administration must report to a contract administrator any meaningful communications they have held directly with the contractor, including any information that might potentially affect the performance, price, cost or any other contract requirements. Meaningful communications help control actions that are otherwise inconsistent with contract requirements.

- As stated in FAR 42.402, the contract administration office (CAO) will make the necessary arrangements in order to eliminate duplicative reviews, requests, investigations, and audits.

Notifications should include:

(1) Visitors' names, official positions, and security clearances.

(2) Date and duration of the visit.

(3) Name and address of contractor and personnel to be contacted.

(4) Contract number, program involved, and purpose of visit.

(5) If desired, visitors to a contractor's plant may request that a representative of the CAO accompany them. In any event, the CAO has final authority to decide whether a representative shall accompany a visitor.

The CAO shall be fully informed of any agreements reached with the contractor or any other results of the visit that may affect the CAO.

- Periodically review the roles and responsibilities with the Contracting Officers' Representatives (CORs) to ensure they are properly performing duties within the limits of their authority, within the time limits established in the contract, and in compliance with FAR 42.1104, which states the following:

In performing surveillance, Contract Administration Office personnel shall avoid any action that may:

- Be inconsistent with any contract requirement; or
- Result in claims of waivers, of changes, or of other contract modifications.

Monitoring may uncover more direct evidence of problems, such as requests for change orders from the contractor, and invoice or voucher items or amounts that are not consistent with contract requirements. The earlier contract administration problems are identified, the easier it will be to resolve them. Contracts at or below the simplified acquisition threshold should not normally require production surveillance.

Requests and Feedback on Contractor Performance

A considerable amount of time in administering a contract is dedicated to responding to the contractor's request for either approval or some other Government action. The Contracting Officer must correctly identify the contract clause (if any) that authorizes the request and appropriate response.

There are clauses that contain instructions for the contractor and the Government and specific time restraints for certain actions.

Example: FAR 52.243-1 Changes clause states that the contractor must assert its right to an adjustment within 30 days from the date of the receipt of the written (change) order. However, if the Contracting Officer decides that the facts justify it, the Contracting Officer may receive and act upon a proposal submitted before final payment of the contract.

This example demonstrates the need, not only for the response but also the requirement for the timeliness of the response.

Example: FAR 52.222-2 Overtime Premiums clause states that the contractor must request and receive approval prior to encountering overtime payments. Neither the clause nor the prescription provides a specific timeframe for when the request and approval must occur.

This example demonstrates the need to determine what constitutes a timely response (normally an agreed amount of time between the contractor and the Government).

Inspection

FAR 52.2 ** *Inspection clause* *acquisition.gov*

The specific inspection clause in the contract contains requirements for the contractor based upon the approval of the Government. There are four basic types of inspection requirements.

Government Reliance on Inspection by the Contractor (Non-commercial): FAR 52.246-1, Contractor Inspection Requirements, is the standard clause used to identify this quality level. The clause is required for use for supplies or services when the contract amount does not exceed the simplified acquisition threshold, unless the Contracting Officer decides that some form of Government inspection and testing is necessary, per FAR 46.301. The clause does allow some specialized Government inspection and testing but relies on the contractor for an overall inspection.

Government Reliance on Inspection by the Contractor (Commercial): FAR 52.212-4, Contract Terms and Conditions-Commercial Items, includes inspection and acceptance for commercial items/supplies. It states that the contractor will only tender those items or services that conform to the requirements of the contract. It further elaborates that the Government reserves the right to inspect or test any supplies or services that have been tendered for acceptance.

Standard Inspection Requirement: The standard inspection clause, FAR 52.246-2, Inspection of Supplies—Fixed-Price, requires that the contractor establish and maintain an inspection system not otherwise defined, except that it must be acceptable to the Government. The standard inspection clause can be the only inspection clause in a contract, or it can be the foundation for other Government inspection specifications. The FAR specifies other clauses for use with different contract types and in specific situations. With minor adjustments in wording for contract type and applications, these are basically the same as the standard inspection clause.

Higher-Level Quality Control Requirement: FAR 52.246-11, Higher-Level Contract Quality Requirement (Government Specification), is the clause used when the technical requirements of a contract mandate closer control of work processes or attention to such factors as planning. This type of clause requires the contractor to comply with Government inspection or quality assurance procedures if such is described in the contract. An example of a higher-level quality control standard is ISO 9000, as stated in FAR 46.202-4.

Contracts —
- Firm fixed price (of service contracts)
- Cost – reimbursement (of developmental/proof of concept contracts).
- Time-/ material / labor-hour.

International Organization for Standardization (ISO) 9000

Introduction

There may be a contract requirement for the contractor to adhere to ISO 9000 for its quality control. The CO must ensure that the COR is familiar with ISO 9000 relative to any requests and/or approvals that may be required.

What is ISO 9000?

ISO 9000 standards for ensuring quality control were originally developed by the International Organization for Standardization (ISO). There are multiple standards covered in the ISO 9000 family, including:

- ISO 9001:2008 - requirements of a quality management system
- ISO 9000:2005 - basic concepts and language
- ISO 9004:2009 - making quality management system more efficient
- ISO 19011:2011 - guidance for internal and external audits of quality management systems

The ISO 9000 series is based on eight quality management principles. The type of organization, its product, and its specific situation will dictate how they are implemented.

Principle 1 – Customer focus
Principle 2 – Leadership
Principle 3 – Involvement of people
Principle 4 – Process approach
Principle 5 – System approach to management
Principle 6 – Continual improvement
Principle 7 – Factual approach to decision making
Principle 8 – Mutually beneficial supplier relationships

ISO 9000 vs. agency standards

In some agencies, the ISO 9000 is used in lieu of agency standards. The intent is to allow contractors maximum flexibility in establishing efficient and effective quality programs that meet contractual requirements.

Becoming ISO 9000 certified

In order for a company to become ISO certified, it must go through the registration process of application, document review, assessment, registration, and surveillance. Once approved, the registration is generally valid for three years. Periodic surveillance audits are performed to ensure continued compliance with the quality system.

First Article Testing

First Article Testing (FAT) means testing and evaluating the first article for conformance with specified contract requirements before or in the initial stage of production.

The Contracting Officer is also responsible for performing duties related to First Article Testing. In accordance with FAR 9.307, before the contractor sends the first article report to the Government activity accountable for approval at the address designated in the contract, the CAO shall furnish that activity with as much advance notification as is possible of the shipment, and:

> (1) Advise that activity of the contractual requirements for testing and approval, or evaluation, as appropriate;

> (2) Call attention to the notice requirement in paragraph (b) of the clause at 52.209-3, First Article Approval—Contractor Testing, or 52.209-4, First Article Approval—Government Testing; and

> (3) Request that the activity inform the contract administration office of the date when testing or evaluation will be completed.

Feedback on Contractor Performance

In addition to monitoring the actions of Government officials, the CAO must obtain sufficient data to verify satisfactory performance by the contractor. The COR must be able to recognize any evidence of potential performance problems by either the contractor or the Government.

Daily logs or progress reports required by a contract administration plan or the contract often provide early warning indicators of potential changes, delays, or other problems in contractor performance. Government officials or the contractor may provide reports. The required submission of written data from a contractor must be covered by a contract requirement. Since the needs of different contracts vary widely, there are no standard FAR clauses addressing content requirements for progress reports.

CORs may initiate written reports identifying potential or actual delays in performance. They should be advised to provide such reports with sufficient time for necessary action by the contracting office and with a specific recommendation for action. The required submission of written data from a contractor must be covered by a contract. However, some well-timed questions may produce valuable oral information. If the requested information is not simple enough to be answered by a brief question-and-answer session, it probably should have had a contract submission requirement to fulfill that need.

Progress Report Reviews and Actions

Progress reports are long-term monitoring reviews used by the CAO to observe a contractor's performance. The CAO has to review the contractor's progress reports, and then has to provide comments to the Contracting Officer within four working days. If the report states that the contractor's performance is on-schedule and the CAO agrees, the CAO does not have to add comments. In other cases, the CAO has to include comments and recommend corrective actions.

The fact that a monthly progress report is required from the contractor and/or the COR does not relieve the contractor of the obligation to report anticipated or actual delays to the COR or the contracting office as soon as such delays are recognized. Once an initial analysis is made and reported, the contractor does not need to repeat the analysis in regularly scheduled progress reports, but progress toward correction must be tracked if a correction was indicated in the analysis.

Production Progress Reports

Production progress reports are generally required unless the work is performed under a Federal Supply Schedule (FSS), a construction contract, or a facilities contract. In FAR 52.242-2, Production Progress Reports, it states that delays in furnishing production reports allow the Contracting Officer to withhold from payment an amount not exceeding $25,000 or 5% of the total contract amount, whichever is less. Some production contracts require a phased schedule for reporting progress. There is no standard format, but these schedules are often characterized by reporting associated with various stages of the production cycle, such as purchasing, tooling, component manufacture, and shipping.

Research and Development (R&D), Scientific and Technical Reports

Since the primary purpose of Research and Development (R&D) contracts is to advance scientific and technical knowledge, they represent some unique monitoring problems. The Government must monitor technical progress closely. Therefore, progress reports are often required from the contractor and may include:

- Number and names of key personnel working on the project during the reporting period
- The direction of the work
- Negative results of work or experimentation
- Problems encountered
- Efforts were taken to resolve problems in terms of costs, schedules, and technical objectives

FAR Part 8 Required Sources of Supplies and Services

The Contracting Officer must resolve problems resulting from the shipment, receiving, inspection, and acceptance of deliverables from a FAR 8 sources. These sources include:

- Federal Supply Schedule contractors
- Federal Prison Industries, Inc.
- Javits-Wagner-O'Day Act (JWOD) participating nonprofit agencies

[handwritten: Ability - 1 / non-profit. Committee oversees performance]

In solving issues involving FAR 8 sources, the contracting office will follow the procedures in FAR Part 8 as listed next:

[handwritten: somewhere 13% then CDC → GSA → maintains contracts (supply schedule monitory)]

- Federal Supply Schedule supplies inspection and acceptance (FAR 8.405-2).
  (1) Consignees shall inspect supplies at destination except when—
      (i) The schedule contract indicates that mandatory source inspection is required by the schedule contracting agency; or
      (ii) A schedule item is covered by a product description, and the ordering activity determines that the schedule contracting agency's inspection assistance is needed (based on the ordering volume, the complexity of the supplies, or the past performance of the supplier).
  (2) When the schedule contracting agency performs the inspection, the ordering activity will provide two copies of the order specifying source inspection to the schedule contracting agency. The contracting agency will notify the ordering activity of acceptance or rejection of the supplies.
  (3) Material inspected at source by the schedule contracting agency, and determined to conform to the product description of the schedule, shall not be re-inspected for the same purpose. The consignee shall limit inspection to kind, count, and condition on receipt.
  (4) Unless otherwise provided in the schedule contract, acceptance is conclusive, except as regards latent defects, fraud, or such gross mistakes as amount to fraud.
- JWOD agency compliance with orders (FAR 8.705-4)
- JWOD agency shipping (FAR 8.708)
- JWOD agency quality of merchandise (FAR 8.710)
- Quality complaints about JWOD supplies or services (FAR 8.711)
- Specification changes for JWOD items (FAR 8.712)
- JWOD central nonprofit agency addresses (FAR 8.714)

The addresses of the central nonprofit agencies are:

(1) National Industries for the Blind, 1310 Braddock Place, Alexandria, VA 22314-1691, (703) 310-0500; and

(2) NISH, 8401 Old Courthouse Road, Vienna, VA 22182, (571) 226-4660.

Breaches of Contract

Careful monitoring of a contract pays dividends in the early identification of performance problems. Various problems can occur, and some of these problems involve one party potentially breaking a promise, technically referred to as a breach. A breach of contract is a failure, without legal excuse, to perform any promise that forms the whole or part of a contract. A breach occurs when:

A party to a contract fails to perform, either in whole or in part

- Gives notice beforehand that it will not perform the contract when the time for performance arrives (constructive breach)
- A party makes performance impossible for itself or the other party

Every breach of contract gives the injured party the right to pursue and collect damages. The party harmed by a breach may sometimes, in addition to pursuing and collecting damages, be excused from its performance responsibilities. The Government can be guilty of a breach when it issues a unilateral change to a contract that is outside the scope of the contract or fails to disclose pertinent site information for onsite work.

The contractor can be guilty of a breach when it abandons contract performance or commits a fraudulent act in connection with a contract.

- To avoid a breach of contract, the Contracting Officer should:
- Verify and record evidence of actual or potential performance problems, constructive changes, or other breaches by first correctly identifying the terms and conditions at issue, if any.
- Contact the contractor to obtain an understanding of the problem, and only contact those individuals necessary to verify evidence.
- Make sure the information provided identifies both the symptoms and causes of any potential problems.
- Identify and obtain corrections to any Government report (progress reports, inspection reports, etc.) and inform the requiring activity.

There may be a need to conduct fact-finding with the officials involved in a problem to identify its symptoms and cause. Methods the Contracting Officer may use to gather these facts include:

- Discussions with the contractor
- Personal observations at the worksite
- Discussions with a COR
- Discussions with quality assurance personnel

In order to verify and document evidence of actual or potential performance problems, constructive changes, or other breaches, the Contracting Officer will perform fact-finding as stated above. Information from the COR and the quality assurance personnel provide valuable indicators of any actual or potential performance problems and/or constructive changes. The data supporting the inspection and acceptance methods utilized in the contract are provided in respective reports, (i.e., inspection, acceptance, scheduling, and approval submittals).

Acceptance

The place of acceptance is specified in the contract, as stated in FAR 46.503. If the quality assurance occurs at the source of origin, then acceptance is ordinarily at the source. If quality assurance occurs at the destination, acceptance is ordinarily at the destination. There may be occasions when the Government does not inspect and accept the supplies and/or services in a timely manner. In such instances, implied acceptance has occurred. In other words, implied acceptance occurs when the Government fails to notify the contractor of its rejection within a reasonable time after delivery or completion. The length of time that is reasonable depends upon the nature of the supplies, the difficulty of inspection, and the impact of the delay upon the contractor. Acceptance also is conditioned upon latent and/or patent defects. The following definitions are provided: *Defects:*

- Latent defects are defects that existed at the time of Government acceptance but could not be discovered by a reasonable inspection (FAR 2.101)
- Patent defects are any defects which exist at the time of acceptance and are not a latent defect. (FAR 46.101)

Supplies and/or services should not be accepted when they do not conform to all aspects of the contract requirement. FAR 46.101 states that non-conforming supplies or services can be classified into the next three categories:

Categories	Characteristics
Critical Non-conformance.	A nonconformance that is likely to result in hazardous or unsafe conditions for individuals using, maintaining, or depending upon the supplies or services. Is likely to prevent the performance of a vital agency mission.
Major Non-conformance.	A non-conformance, other than critical that is likely to result in failure of the supplies or services. Or to materially reduce the usability of the supplies or services for their intended purpose.
Minor Non-conformance	A non-conformance that is not likely to materially reduce the usability of the supplies or services for their intended purpose, or is a departure from established standards having little bearing on the effective use or operation of the supplies or services.

SME / Technical Monitor ⟶ COR → CS → CO

Contract Non-conformance

The Government has the absolute right to insist upon strict adherence to the contractual requirements. No matter how slight a defect, the Government is entitled to reject an item if it does not conform to all the specifications, as stated in the contract. Normally, the Government will reject a product that does not conform to the contract requirements when that nonconformance adversely affects safety, health, reliability, durability, performance, interchangeability, or any other basic objective of the requirement.

The Contracting Officer shall ordinarily reject supplies/services when non-conformance is critical or major. However, there may be circumstances when acceptance of such non-conformity is in the best interests of the Government. Any time a non-conforming supply or service is being considered for acceptance, approval must be authorized by the requiring activity (customer). These circumstances include reasons of economy or urgency. As stated in FAR 46.407, determinations of non-conformance will be based upon:

- The advice of the technical activity that the item is safe to use and will perform its intended purpose;
- Information regarding the nature and extent of the nonconformance or otherwise incomplete supplies or services;
- A request from the contractor for acceptance of the non-conforming or otherwise incomplete supplies or services (if feasible);
- A recommendation for acceptance, conditional acceptance, or rejection, with supporting rationale; and
- The contract adjustment considered appropriate, including any adjustment offered by the contractor.

The Contracting Officer shall obtain the concurrence of the responsible technical activity and the responsible health official when health factors are involved. The Contracting Officer also should hold periodic site meetings with requiring activity and end users to obtain, as well as provide, pertinent information on a contract's status. These meetings help foster a team approach to contract administration.

Periodic meetings can be held onsite with the contractor and Government technical personnel who have contract administration responsibility. The goal is not only to identify potential change situations but also to obtain monitoring data through observations. Onsite meetings allow the Government and contractor personnel to identify, as well as resolve, technical problems at the operating level.

Determine Potential Impact

The key to effective, innovative problem-solving techniques is not merely to search for textbook or regulatory solutions. Proactive problem-solving techniques involve:

- Careful thought
- A sense of practicality
- A positive approach (whenever possible)

The Contracting Officer should consult regulatory guidance to ascertain what may be required as a function of contractual terms and conditions. A performance problem is any known, unknown, or predictable situation that may endanger or disrupt the efficient execution of a contract's terms and conditions, regardless of whether the situation was or may be caused by the contractor, the Government, or both.

When a performance problem occurs, the potential impact on cost, delivery, and other requirements must be determined. When an actual or potential performance problem is identified, and it is not just a simple matter of clarifying a contract's requirement, a determination must be made concerning the problem's significance.

The overriding issue is the extent of damage the Government will incur if the problem is not resolved. The amount of time and effort required to resolve the problem has a direct relationship to the problem's significance to the end user's requirements. Factors that should be considered are:

- Delivery
- Price
- Quantity
- Quality

When a serious problem surfaces, one of the first issues to consider is whether the contractor should continue performance. From the evidence gathered, the Contracting Officer should be able to determine the seriousness of the problem, in addition to the amount of time correction of the problem will take. Another consideration the Contracting Officer should take into account is whether it will be more costly to the Government to pay additional money and suspend/stop the work until the correction is completed or pay for the correction to be made later.

Problem Resolution

The Contracting Officer should attempt to reach an informal resolution before invoking formal procedures, i.e., a cure or show cause notice. The informal remedies available are:

- An informal agreement on a corrective resolution
- A memorandum of concern to request a written plan from the contractor for correcting performance, including:
  - Statement of the problem
  - Need for corrective action
  - Response time
  - Place for a contractor to sign acknowledging receipt
  - A contract modification (with consideration if applicable)

Excusable Delays

If the contractor claims that a pending or actual delay is excusable, investigate and resolve the issue of whether the delay is excusable under the applicable contract clause. For a commercial item under FAR 52.212-4, the contractor is not responsible for delays caused by an occurrence beyond its reasonable control, such as:

- Acts of God or the public enemy
- Acts of the Government in its sovereign or contractual capacity
- Fires or floods
- Epidemics
- Quarantine restrictions
- Strikes, unusually severe weather
- Delays of common carriers

If there is a need to stop work while the problem is being resolved, the Contracting Officer will follow the procedures for stop-work orders or suspension of work in FAR 52.242-14.

Documenting the File

In order to track the contractor's performance for later use as past performance data, the Contracting Officer will document the contract file concerning:

1. Monitoring activities
2. Evidence of actual or potential performance problems, constructive changes, or other breaches
3. Any actions taken to resolve potential performance problems, constructive changes, or other breaches

Summary

The keys to successful contract administration during the performance phase are knowledge, communication, and documentation. You should assume that your contractor is willing and able to perform in accordance with the terms and conditions of the contract until, and at such time, that the opposite proves to be the case. A proactive teaming approach can resolve many difficulties before they negatively influence the product or service the customer expects to receive.

Notes

Notes

Notes

Chapter 2 - Contract Administration Planning

Introduction

The two principal objectives of contract administration planning are:

1. To establish a system that reinforces the performance of both parties' (both buyer and seller) responsibilities

2. To provide means for the early recognition of performance problems either before or when they occur

How the contract will be administered is an acquisition planning phase consideration, with the finalization of a plan occurring after the contract has been awarded. The results of contract planning are reflected in the contract administration plan. Not all contracts require a formal contract administration plan. The requirements for contract administration plans are based on individual agency's policies and procedures.

For commercial items or services, little contract administration will be needed, and therefore, the plan should be simple and straightforward. Large and complex acquisitions and non-commercial contracts will require more detailed plans, and contract administration will require a considerable effort by both the Government and the contractor.

The specific nature and extent of contract administration vary from contract to contract. It can range from the minimum acceptance of delivery and payment to the contractor to extensive involvement by program, audit, and procurement personnel throughout the contract term.

Factors influencing the degree of contract administration will include:

- The nature of the work
- Type of contract awarded
- The experience and commitment of the personnel involved

Failure to read and understand a contract frequently results in contract administration problems. When contract administration monitoring or surveillance systems are planned, they must be designed to ensure that the Government and a contractor can live up to their promises and fulfill responsibilities. The primary concern of the contract professional during contract planning is avoiding problems and setting up systems to mitigate the risk to both the Government and the contractor when problems surface.

Contract Administration Planning

The key to effective contract management is a flexible contract administration plan. The steps in planning for contract administration follow:

INPUT: A contract and contact with technical and other support personnel

1. Determine the required level of contract surveillance.
2. Determine what contract administration functions (if any) will be delegated.
3. Determine contract administration as applicable.
4. Develop a contract administration plan.
5. Identify qualified personnel (as authorized and necessary) to represent the Contracting Officer in administering contract requirements.
6. Notify the contractor of personnel authorized to represent the Contracting Officer in administering contract requirements.

Level of Contract Surveillance

When the contracting office receives a contract for administration, the contract professional first reviews the contract file. To familiarize yourself with the contract clauses and requirements, your first step in contract administration is to review the pre-award file documentation, especially when another contracting office awarded the contract. For instance, there may be questions regarding the interpretation of an agency-specific contract clause or the minutes from the pre-proposal meeting that may include some pertinent information regarding specific requirements.

Some other contract file areas of prime importance are:

- The assignment of contract administration functions
- Criticality designator and security requirements
- Production surveillance requirements and reporting
- Supporting contract administration requirements
- Other special contract requirements (when applicable)

After completing a review of the contract file, all critical areas bearing on performance and monitoring should be identified. With this knowledge, the contracting professional can determine how critical the requirement is to the Government and how much time and effort are needed to ensure successful contract administration.

The contractor is responsible for timely contract performance. The Government will maintain surveillance of contractor performance as necessary to protect its interest. When the contracting office retains a contract for administration, the Contracting Officer administering the contract determines the extent of surveillance.

To determine the extent of performance monitoring, the Contracting Officer will:

1. Meet with the requiring activity to discuss performance monitoring. The Contracting Officer should meet with the requiring activity to discuss requirements for contract administration. This discussion should include sharing any acquisition history concerning the contractor and the required supplies or services. The Contract Professional will focus the discussion regarding contract monitoring on the requiring activity's priorities, ensure the Government is working as a team, and foster understanding of the priorities and potential problem areas.

2. Assess factors that indicate the appropriate monitoring level. The Contract Administration Office will determine the monitoring level. Many factors, as stated in FAR 42.1104, are involved in determining how much monitoring is necessary for the contract. Some of these factors to consider are the criticality of the requirement as assigned by the Contracting Officer, the contract performance schedule, and the contractors' history of contract performance. Most customary commercial practices may not require contract administration in the acquisition of a commercial item.

When acquiring commercial items, the Government relies on the contractor's existing quality assurance systems as a substitute for Government inspection and testing before delivery, unless customary market practices for what is being acquired include an in-process inspection. If such inspection is customary, the Government's inspection must be consistent with commercial practices. However, the Government will never waive its right to inspect and accept an item if it will prejudice its other rights under the acceptance paragraph in FAR 52.212-4, Contract Terms and Conditions-Commercial Items. The Government must not rely on inspection by the contractor if the contracting office determines that the Government has a need to test what is being acquired before delivery or passing judgment on the adequacy of the contractor's internal work processes. Standard Government clauses specify the type of inspection system that the contractor must maintain for the performance of the contract. Some of the contract clauses include:

- FAR 52.246-1, Contractor Inspection Requirements, relies on the contractor's own internal inspection procedures and industry standards.
- FAR 52.246-2, Inspection Supplies—Fixed Price, requires a contractor to establish and maintain an inspection system undefined except that it must be acceptable to the Government. This standard clause can be the only inspection clause in a contract, or it can be the foundation upon which other Government inspection specifications are based. It contains the Government's basic rights of inspection.
- FAR 52.246-11, Higher-Level Contract Quality Requirement (Government Specification) requires a contractor to comply with a specific Government inspection system or quality control system or quality program.

The Government can only require the contractor to submit data for monitoring purposes as specified in the initial contract. Any required data must be specifically authorized within the schedule, specification, or by a contract clause. Therefore, it is important to determine, upfront, what type of inspection system is required by the contract to decide whether you want to rely solely on it for monitoring a contractor's performance.

A contract is basically an instrument that allocates and defines risks and responsibilities between the contracting parties. Its terms and conditions set forth each party's obligations, as well as each party's rights if the other should fail to carry out its obligations. The Contract Professional should understand how the standard and unique terms and conditions, as stated in the contract, affect the contractor's risks. Once the Contract Professional can identify the risk and understand what the contractor might do to protect their interest, then the appropriate monitoring level necessary to protect the Government's interests can be established.

Numerous techniques and procedures exist for determining whether satisfactory delivery or contract completion will take place. They include reliance on the contractor's inspection system, 100 percent inspection, sample inspection, inspection by exception, monitoring production or delivery schedules, and monitoring schedules devised by Government personnel to measure contract performance.

The Criticality

The Contracting Officer is required to assign a designator, prior to award, based on the criticality of the requirement for all contracts. Criticality refers to the degree of overall importance that a contract has to the Government and will be indicated on the contract. The criticality designators indicate where to concentrate on surveillance efforts. These designators become particularly important when contract administration resources are spread thin. FAR 42.1105, Assignment of Criticality Designators requires the choice of either "A," "B," or "C." The criterion for each of these designators is shown in the following table.

Criticality Designators	
Criticality Designator	**Criterion**
A	Critical contracts, including DX-rated contracts, contracts containing an unusual or compelling urgency, and contracts for major systems.
B	Contracts (other than those designated "A") for items needed to maintain a Government or contractor production or repair line, to preclude out-of-stock conditions, or to meet user needs for non-stock items.
C	All contracts are other than those designated "A" or "B."

Identify Previous Issues and Problems

Consideration must be given to the amount of time and effort that will be necessary to ensure successful contract performance. This depends on such factors as:

- Type of contract
- Past experiences with this type of requirement
- Past experience with the contractor
- Type of specifications
- Type of requirement
- Warranty provisions
- The urgency of the requirement

An important source of information for identifying potential problem areas is a contractor's performance history in the contract file.

Review the Contractor's Performance History

The data included in the contractor's past performance file is considered confidential and not available to non-Government personnel. Such files should include the following information:

- Past or previous contracts awarded and dollar amounts
- Items/services purchased
- Key personnel involved with the contract
- Delivery/performance results
- Contractor-provided past performance information

The Contractor's Performance History file represents a history of the contractor's performance over a period of time on individual contracts if one exists, plus other information on the contractor's past performance from other sources. This information may be provided by both Government and non-Government sources.

If the Contracting Office has had previous experience with the contractor, past performance problem areas would be documented within this file. These areas will require special attention on a current contract to ensure past performance deficiencies do not continue and are not demonstrated in future work. Deficiencies in a contractor's performance could include:

- Missed delivery dates
- Shortfalls in technical performance capabilities
- Financial difficulties

Review Other Available Indicators of Past Performance

Normally, records of past performance within the contracting office will be sufficient for planning efforts. If the Contracting Office has not had any previous experience with the contractor, the Contract Professional may want to look for other indicators of past performance. The contract file itself is the best place to look for other indicators. Past performance or responsibility determination data in the contract file may contain information from other Government offices, and/or a contractor's commercial clients. Therefore, it is imperative that Contract Professionals keep information provided by both Government and non-Government personnel strictly confidential.

According to FAR 42.1503, agency evaluations of contractor performance prepared under this subpart shall be provided to the contractor as soon as practicable after completion of the evaluation. Contractors are given at least 30 days to respond or provide additional information. The completed evaluation shall be presented to Government personnel and the contractor whose performance is being examined. A copy of the annual or final past performance evaluation shall be provided to the contractor as soon as it is finalized.

The Government needs to monitor only timely delivery or performance and inspect the delivered items or work performed. In coordinating a surveillance method for a contract, according to FAR 42.1104, the contract administration office should make use of and rely on the contractor's inspection system, data management system, or production control system.

The goal of contract monitoring is to unveil actual or potential default situations and the need for Government action. The Contract Professional needs to be proactive, and act promptly and carefully to initiate immediate improvements while preserving the Government's right to future remedies available under the contract. Although Government action may supplement— but not supplant the contractor's own efforts to solve performance problems— the Contract Professional needs to be aware of what Government action will be required as early as possible.

Determine Which Contract Administration Functions Will Be Delegated

The Contracting Officer is the official authorized to enter into, administer, and terminate contracts. The CO also can make related determinations and findings. A single CO may be responsible for delegating duties to specialized Contracting Officers.

Termination Contracting Officer (TCO)

The official authorized to perform post-award actions limited to the termination of contracts.

Administrative Contracting Officer (ACO)

The official authorized to perform any post-award contractual action assigned by the CO. Some agencies have set up separate offices called a Contract Administrative Office (CAO) to handle post-award, functions as prescribed by that agency. An Administrative Contracting Officer would be assigned to the CAO.

> *Note: For purposes of clarity, all text references to a "Contracting Officer" refer to the Procurement Contracting Officer (PCO), that is, the CO responsible for all duties, regardless of whether those duties have been delegated to other Contracting Officers. The PCO can be the ACO in a cradle-to-grave situation.*

The term "cradle-to-grave" simply means the contracting office responsible for the pre-award and award will also be responsible for the administration of the contract. There are some advantages in doing this. For instance, if the same Contract Professionals were involved throughout the contracting process, they would be very familiar with the history of the contract and all of its intricacies.

On the other hand, there is the option of having the contract administration done by an Administrative Contracting Officer located at a Contract Administration Office.

One advantage of the delegation of administration is that the contracting personnel have in-depth experience in the administration phase, and have experts to assist in areas such as property administration. However, there are certain functions that cannot be delegated and must remain the responsibility of the PCO.

Learner Reference

Functions That Cannot Be Delegated By the PCO

- Award, agree to, or execute a contract
- Authorize work outside the scope of the contract
- Authorize a constructive change
- Obligate, in any way, the payment of money by the Government
- Give direction to the contractor, except as provided in the contract, or as modified
- Resolve any dispute concerning a question of law or fact arising under the contract
- Re-delegate any assigned duties unless specifically authorized to do so
- Cause the contractor to incur costs not specifically covered by the contract with the expectation that such costs will be reimbursed by the Government

Contract Administration Decision

The Contracting Officer (CO) determines how contract administration will be handled. The CO must determine whether to:

- Retain the contract and perform all applicable contract administration functions
- Retain the contract and perform administrative functions with the assistance of other Government personnel
- Assign the contract to a Contract Administration Office (CAO)
- Assign the contract to a CAO with specific limitations and/or specific additions

Delegation of Contract Administration

In assigning a contract for administration by a CAO, the contracting office may specifically delegate functions in addition to the 70 normal functions. These additional 11 functions, listed in FAR 42.302, can be performed when and to the magnitude precisely authorized by the contracting office. These functions, unless specifically assigned, cannot be performed by the CAO.

The contracting office also may withhold any of the FAR-specified functions when either the Contracting Officer determines the contracting office can better handle the performance of the function(s), or it is required by agency regulations or interagency cross-servicing agreements. Any decision to withhold administrative functions should be made after consulting with the CAO.

Tailor the Assignment of Functions and CAO Support

Some of the Contract Administrator functions may not even be applicable to the contract involved, such as monitoring industrial labor relations matters on a contract for commercial products or maintaining surveillance of flight operations on a contract that does not involve aircraft.

There are also functions that are dependent on events that occur during contract performance. For example, the contracting office may have the responsibility of negotiating supplemental agreements and/or changing contract delivery schedules. However, if no change in contract delivery schedules is required during contract performance, then this function will not be performed.

The CAO also has the authority to request supporting contract administration from another CAO for any function that has been assigned by the CO. The CAO can even reassign the contract when another office is in a better position to perform administrative functions. The CO may recall a contract or function previously assigned for administration when warranted by a change in circumstances, and approved by a higher level.

Develop a Contract Administration Plan

Although the FAR does not require the preparation of a formal contract administration plan, the CO is responsible for ensuring that the parties have complied with all terms and conditions of the contract.

A formal contract administration plan is essential when the contract involves large dollar amounts or complex technical requirements. Such contracts typically place many duties and responsibilities on both parties. Such a plan should be implemented immediately after award. The plan should provide for an appropriate level of surveillance or monitoring of contractor performance and timely and proper performance of the Government's responsibilities. Each agency has its own specific requirement for contract administration plans.

Although finalized at contract award, the contract administration plan needs to be a flexible, living document to fulfill its purpose of providing a baseline for project management and scheduling. An effective plan is a simple way of tracking the extent of contract completion and can be an invaluable tool in your preparation for the post-award orientation conference.

As contract performance progresses, it may be necessary to shift responsibilities or add tasks that could not have been anticipated at the time of award. Over the life of the contract, therefore, a contract administration plan may require periodic updates or changes.

Identify Contract Terms and Conditions Related to Administration

Classify and outline all major tasks that arise from the terms and conditions of the contract. The process may be enhanced by dividing it into four parts:

- Administration preliminaries (e.g., delegations of responsibility and the post-award orientation conference)
- Contract performance (e.g., monitoring payment provisions)
- Inspection and acceptance
- Post-contract activity (e.g., duties under warranty provisions, contract close-out). After you have reviewed your contract and identified major tasks for your checklist, go through some of the items listed in the following table of common contract administration functions to see if there are others you wish to include

Learner Reference

There is no universal format that must be followed in preparing a contract administration plan. At a minimum, it should cover all issues necessary to ensure that all parties understand their roles and suspense dates for assigned tasks. It should be kept as simple and precise as possible. A sample format is shown next, listing possible tasks included in a contract administration plan (if applicable).

Typical Contract Administration Plan Format

- Title of the contract, related identifiers, and criticality designator.
- The identity of the contractor and key contractor personnel.
- Location of files on the contract and the contractor.
- A brief description of the work to be performed.
- Place of performance and/or delivery points.
- Reporting requirements.
- The contractor's milestones for such critical events as:
  - First article testing and reporting.
  - Performance or delivery.
  - Submission of progress reports.
  - Submission of invoices/vouchers and other data related to payment.
- The identity of the CO's Representative (COR).
- Tasks to be performed by Government personnel and milestones for each task for such functions as:
  - Monitoring the contractor's quality assurance program.
  - Furnishing Government property and monitoring its use.
  - Reviewing and responding to contractor reports/requests.
  - Receiving, inspecting, and accepting the work.
  - Certifying costs incurred or physical progress for payment purposes.
  - Monitoring compliance with the small business subcontracting plan.
- Tasks delegated to each COR (including any limits on their authority).
- Potential problem areas.

Contract administration planning is an important process and must be performed by the ACO once the contract is assigned to CAO. It involves setting up systems and procedures to ensure compliance with a contract's terms and conditions during performance.

The goal of the contract administration planning is to identify:

1. What must be done
2. When it must take place
3. Who must do it
4. How it is to be accomplished
5. Where it is to be accomplished

After the contract administration planning is completed, you should start preparing for the post-award meeting.

Team Concept

The Contracting Officer usually heads up the contract administration team. Contract Administrators and Contract Professionals generally assist the Contracting Officer in performing this role. At FAR 2.101, the definition of a Contracting Officer, "...includes certain authorized representatives of the Contracting Officer acting within the limits of their authority as delegated by the Contracting Officer." Pursuant to Government policies and procedures, Contracting Officers are responsible for:

- Designating properly trained CORs prior to contract award
- Nominating, tracking, and managing CORs
- Maintaining records for each COR appointed
- Providing performance input to the COR's supervisor
- Monitoring contractor performance overseen by CORs

The Contracting Officer's Representative (COR), serves as the eyes and ears of the CO and usually does not have contracting authority. A COR is appointed by the PCO via a designation letter that contains instructions and outlines specific responsibilities in relation to the contractual document.

A COR is usually a person with proper training and expertise in the area of the contracted effort, possessing the necessary background to monitor technical aspects of contract performance. Typical primary responsibilities of a COR include:

- Monitoring performance
- Evaluating work as it progresses
- Exercising appropriate technical direction within the scope of the contract
- Inspecting and accepting completed work for the Government

The roles and authorities of these team players depend on the size of the Government organization and the complexity of the contract. Some typical responsibilities of key contract administration personnel are:

- Contracting Officer: The Contracting Officer is principally responsible for the existing business relationship between the Government and a contractor, including analyzing costs and interpreting and implementing contractual terms and conditions.
- Project Inspectors: Project inspectors can report to a Contract Administrator, Contracting Officer, or COR depending on the contract administration plan for each project. Their responsibilities include monitoring and inspection duties, such as reviewing the contractor's progress reports, inspecting all work performed by the contractor for contract compliance, maintaining a list of subcontractors on the project, and if required submitting periodic or daily reports to the Contracting Officer or COR.

Although they may not be specifically designated, the Contracting Officer may request that other Government officials become involved in contract administration functions as necessary. The following list of individuals may provide input as requested and may be available to perform various tasks.

- Program or requiring activity personnel
- Administrative support personnel
- Legal counsel
- Cost and price analysts
- Quality assurance specialists
- Property control administrators
- Small Business Administration

As mentioned previously, the delegation of contract administration responsibilities to key team members should be made in writing. While signed by the Contracting Officer, the designee should countersign the letter of delegation, and a copy of the completed letter should be placed in the contract file.

Post-Award Orientation

Contract administration planning from the PCO and CAO perspective is to ensure that each individual understands his/her roles and duties necessary for successful contract completion. A post-award orientation may be made using a conference, a letter, or other form of written communication. After the contract is awarded, the CAO receives the contract from the PCO and is tasked with establishing a post-award orientation conference to foster this understanding. As stated in FAR 42.501, a post-award orientation aids both the Government and contractor personnel to:

- Achieve a clear and mutual understanding of contract requirements
- Identify and resolve potential problems

It is not, however, a substitute for the contractor to fully understanding the work requirements at the time offers are submitted, nor is it to be used to alter the final agreement arrived at in any negotiations leading to contract award.

Post-award orientation is encouraged to assist small business, small disadvantaged, and women-owned small business concerns.

While cognizant Government or contractor personnel may request the Contracting Officer to arrange a post-award orientation, it is up to the Contracting Officer to decide whether a post-award orientation, in any form, is necessary.

When a post-award orientation is conducted, it should be conducted promptly after the contract award to achieve maximum results. A planned, structured discussion between the Government and the contractor, a post-award orientation focuses on issues, such as:

- Understanding the technical aspects of the contract
- Identifying and resolving oversights
- Preventing problems
- Averting misunderstandings
- Determining how to solve problems that may occur later
- Reaching agreement on common issues

FAR 42.501 states:

a) A post-award orientation aids both Government and contractor personnel to (1) achieve a clear and mutual understanding of all contract requirements, and (2) identify and resolve potential problems. However, it is not a substitute for the contractors fully understanding the work requirements at the time offers are submitted, nor is it to be used to alter the final agreement arrived at in any negotiations leading to contract award.

b) Post-award orientation is encouraged to assist small business; small disadvantaged, women-owned, veteran-owned, HUBZone, and service-disabled-veteran-owned small business concerns (see Part 19).

c) While cognizant Government or contractor personnel may request the Contracting Officer to arrange for orientation, it is up to the Contracting Officer to decide whether a post-award orientation in any form is necessary.

d) Maximum benefits will be realized when orientation is conducted promptly after award.

Learner Reference

Determining the need with the factors in FAR 42.502 in mind, the Contract Administrator must identify and review specific key contract requirements and milestones. These requirements and milestones most likely have been identified in the contract administration plan. These requirements and milestones have been pulled from the Statement of Work, requirements documents, source selection information if applicable, purchase request, and other memoranda and information in the file. The success of a post-award conference rests on the assessment by the Contract Administrator to identify key issues/concerns that could possibly affect contract performance. Hence, the contract administration plan is quite important in identifying possible problems. Post-award orientations are most vital when potential risks to the contractor or the Government have not been addressed within the contract itself. A post-award conference identifies these risks and considers ways of reducing anticipated problems during contract performance.

As stated in FAR 42.502, factors to be considered in determining the need for a post-award orientation include, among other things, the following:

- Type, value, and complexity of the contract
- Complexity and acquisition history of the product or service
- The urgency of the delivery schedule and relationship of the product or service to critical programs
- Extent of subcontracting
- Contractor's performance history and experience with the product or service
- Contractor's status, if any, as a small business, small disadvantaged, women-owned, veteran-owned, HUBZone, or service-disabled-veteran-owned small business concerns
- Safety precautions required for hazardous materials or operations
- Complex financing arrangements, such as progress payments, advance payments, or guaranteed loans

Some common questions to ask in determining the need for a post-award conference include:

- Is this the contractor's first Government contract?
- Has the contractor had little or no previous experience with this type of product or service?
- If the contractor has had previous Government contracts, were an unusual number of problems associated with them?
- Is any aspect of this contract urgent or critical to the Government?
- Does the contract type require a relatively high degree of administration?

There may be a need for a general briefing on one or more aspects of the contract administration. The post-award goals of any contract are to assure that supplies or services are:

- Delivered or performed when and where specified in the contract
- Acceptable in terms of conforming to the contract's specification or statement of work
- Furnished in compliance with other terms and conditions of the contract

Compliance with other terms and conditions includes requirements, such as:

- Security classifications and requirements
- Record-retention requirements
- Service contract act requirements
- Federal and state labor requirements
- Federal policies on nondiscrimination because of age

When the decision is made to hold a conference or conduct some other form of a post-award orientation, there must be additional documentation included in the contract file.

Determine the Type of Orientation

A post-award orientation may be conducted in a face-to-face conference, by a letter, or by a teleconference. Any combination of these formats is acceptable. The ACO makes the final choice.

Usually, a post-award orientation is held as a face-to-face orientation conference when the contractor does not have a clear understanding of the scope of the contract, the technical requirements of the contract or any other rights and obligations of the parties in any area.

Generally, a letter can be used as an alternative to a formal post-award conference when only minor details need to be conveyed to the contractor, and the contractor has had previous experience in producing the items or providing the services, or the procurement is not particularly complex. The letter should identify the Government representative responsible for administering the contract and cite any unusual or significant contract requirements.

A teleconference is usually sufficient when there has been good prior experience with the contractor and matters for discussions are relatively straightforward, or there is no anticipation of problems for good reasons.

A post-award orientation also may represent a combination of these methods. For instance, there may be an uncomplicated procurement with a new contractor. A letter may be sent to convey a few important points, and then followed up with a telephone conference to establish a personal working relationship.

When conducting a conference, the Contracting Officer is responsible for establishing the time and place of the conference. The conference should be held as soon as possible after contract award.

Agenda items may include:

- Providing a copy of the agenda to the contractor and obtaining a response
- Notifying the appropriate Government representatives who will have a significant role interacting with the contractor during performance of the contract and the contractor
- Designating or acting as the chairperson for the orientation conference
- Unless a contract change is contemplated, the chairperson shall emphasize that the contract remains unchanged, unless a modification is issued reflecting such a change
- Conducting a preliminary meeting of Government personnel

It may be useful to hold a preliminary meeting with appropriate Government personnel to ensure that the Government's expectations are clearly expressed and understood. The preliminary meeting will also establish the methodology for handling potential problems that are identified. The Contracting Officer must make all final decisions affecting contract terms and conditions.

Post-award Conference Report

The chairperson is responsible for preparing the report for the post-award orientation conference that serves as documentation for the contract file or the post-award conference report. When documenting this information in the report, any convenient format may be used, providing it contains all the information necessary to document the events of the meeting.

The Contracting Officer, the COR, the contractor, and others as appropriate, should receive copies of the report. A copy should be included in the contract file.

Actions to Resolve Disagreements on Key Issues

Each contractual problem is different, and no single approach can be used to resolve every disagreement that may arise. In general, four steps may be used to resolve points of disagreements on key issues.

Step 1: Fact-Find and Document the contractor's position.

If the problem requires joint contractor/Government problem solving, set up a separate meeting with only those who need to be in attendance as soon as possible.

Take appropriate action to resolve the problem and seek technical or legal advice when necessary.

Step 2: Select the best solution to the problem and seek agreement on it.

Identify if the Contracting Officer should issue a unilateral modification. This action would be the Government's solution to an impasse with a contractor.

If a contract change seems necessary, it must clearly define the extent of proposed change and be implemented promptly. The Contracting Officer must complete and sign a contract modification (SF30) in all cases.

Document the contract file by including in the conference report, as well as all other material, correspondence or follow up actions from the Post-award Orientation in the contract file. In the event of any subsequent disagreements with the contractor, this material can be used to reconstruct facts and events as they occurred. A well-documented contract file will identify and verify the Government's initial position on any performance problems that were anticipated during the orientation or in the early steps of implementation.

Step 3: Provide information on the contract to interested parties.

Provide any documentation to members of the contract administration team as well as the contractor when that information affects their role in contract performance. The Contracting Officer also may receive requests for information from other interested parties, such as other companies that have proposed but were evaluated and determined to be unsuccessful offerors. The release of any information is subject to the requirement of the Freedom of Information Act (FOIA).

Step 4: Obtain executed contractual documents, bonds, or insurance.

Since bonds and certificates of insurance must be executed before performance begins, the deadline for submission should be stated in the contract. It is usually within 10 days after the award. When bonds and certificates are required, request them immediately, normally in the letter accompanying contract award. Reference the contract clause that requires the submission and establish a time for receipt, if the contract does not provide a date.

Summary

This section has hopefully imprinted on you the importance of contract administrative planning. A wise sage once said that "failing to plan is planning to fail." A bit trite, maybe, but so true. As you plan your approach to contract administration for a contract, you are foreseeing problems, aligning resources, and in effect, assuring that the customer receives the required product or service as expected. A written, well-documented administrative plan is your roadmap for success contract administration. You also learned about a Post-award Orientation conference and its importance. By communicating upfront, we can hopefully avoid confusion and conflict later.

Notes

Notes

Notes

Chapter 3 - Monitoring and Documenting Contracto Performance through Metrics

Introduction

Metrics are measures used to indicate progress or achievement and should be considered and developed as part of your contract administrative plan. The variety, level, and quantity of metrics you need to develop for monitoring the contractor's performance will depend on the acquisition. There is no one size that fits all when it comes to metrics. Simple acquisitions may have only a few metrics related to cost, schedule, or performance. The more complex the acquisition, the more complex and numerous the metrics needed to monitor performance. Agency requirements will often dictate specific metrics and their format. Properly administered, metrics can form the documented basis of current contractor performance and establish a baseline for formally rating contractor past performance.

Developing a Metrics Toolbox

Not all data is a metric. Sometimes data is just data. To be considered a metric, data must be correlated, organized, and useful in determining progress or achievement. A good metric will have the following attributes:

- The data elements are available and repeatable
- There is agreement as to what the metric is indicating
- Extended over time, trend analysis can be performed
- The metric drives the right management action

The metrics in your toolbox will change over time, depending on the phase of the acquisition and the usefulness of the particular metric in monitoring performance. The metrics in use must be communicated to all stakeholders, such as buying activity, customer, and the contractor.

Customer Satisfaction

Customer satisfaction is often considered the ultimate metric. Was the customer satisfied with the product or service (i.e., cost, schedule, and performance)? If not, there was a breakdown in the acquisition process, especially if all the other metrics looked good.

Your metric toolbox should include feedback to determine customer satisfaction. Customer feedback can take many forms from formal surveys to telephone calls placed by the Contracting Officer. As with other metrics, the method of obtaining feedback will depend on the complexity and nature of the acquisition.

Rating Past Performance

As stated in FAR 42.1502, regardless of the date of contract award, at the time the work under the contract is completed, agencies shall prepare an evaluation of contractor performance for each contract in excess of limits stated in the section. Exceptions to this are contracts awarded under FAR Subparts 8.6 and 8.7.

In addition, interim evaluations should be prepared as specified by the agencies to provide current information for source selection purposes for a contract with a period of performance, including options, exceeding one year. This evaluation is generally for the entity, division, or unit that performed the contract. The content and format of performance evaluations shall be established in accordance with agency procedures and should be tailored to the size, content, and complexity of the contractual requirements.

General Indicators of Past Performance

Next, are some general indicators of past performance.

- Quality of product or service can be viewed in terms of how well the contractor has complied with contract requirements, and whether it conformed to standards of good workmanship
- Timeliness of performance can be measured in terms of how well the contractor adhered to contract schedules and its responsiveness to technical direction
- Cost control can be evaluated by examining to see if the contractor, among other things, operated at or below budget, submitted reasonably priced change proposals, or provided current, accurate, and complete billings
- Business practices indicate how well the contractor worked with the Contracting Officer and representatives
- Customer satisfaction measures the interface with the ultimate end-user of the product or service

Obtaining Past Performance Data

Generally, the Contracting Officer or the COR will use metric data as detailed in the contract administration plan and record narrative information on such matters as the contractor's:

- Record of conforming to contract requirements and to standards of good workmanship
- Record of forecasting and controlling costs
- Adherence to contract schedules, including the administrative aspects of performance
- History of reasonable and cooperative behavior and commitment to customer satisfaction
- Business-like concern in general for the interest of the customer

Sources of Past Performance Information

Solicit input for the evaluations from the technical office, contracting office, and where appropriate, end-users of the product or service, as stated in FAR 42.15.

Information about a contractor's past performance can come from a variety of sources:

- Reference checks are accomplished by developing a questionnaire that reflects the evaluation rating system that will be used to evaluate offerors using face-to-face interviews, responses returned by mail, telephone interviews, or a combination of these techniques
- Contractor performance evaluations on previous contracts are obtained from agency files or other Federal agencies
- Quality certifications
- Defense Logistics Agency and Defense Contract Audit Agency databases, state and local government offices, and nongovernmental sources as well

Evaluate/Rate Past Performance

Once all the data has been assembled, past performance is evaluated based on the methodology spelled out in the solicitation. Past performance may be rated overall (as a single factor), or there may be several sub-factors with different weights. Ratings are not precise; rather, they are necessarily subjective. There should be sufficient documentation to support the rating.

Learner Reference

Sample Past Performance Report Comments/Ratings	
Category	**Comments**
Quality	"Deliverable items exceed quality standards."
Timeliness	"All scheduled delivery times were met."
Cost Control	"Cost management excellent – 2% under run."
Business Relations	"Not responsive to change procedures."
Customer Satisfaction	"Survey showed over 95% customer satisfaction."
Key Personnel	"Key personnel remained on the project until contract completion."

The sample contractor performance report suggests that each rating area is assigned one of six ratings. Agencies may develop their own.

① CPARS ② "PPARS" ✓ *past performance appraisal retrieval sys*

Contractor Performance Report

Rating		Sample Statement
Unsatisfactory	0	Nonconformance; control problems compromised contract completion.
Poor	1	Responses to administrative requirements were marginally effective.
Fair	2	Excessive workarounds required to meet schedule.
Good	3	Approach to service and technical issues were timely and adequate.
Excellent	4	No quality, cost control, or administrative problems.
Excellent plus	+	Exceptional performance in all rated areas. (Excellent plus, or its equivalent, should be reserved for truly exceptional actions.)

(handwritten margin notes: "Rubric", "5-point scale")

Contractor Feedback

As stated in FAR 42.1503, the contractor should be provided copies of the agency evaluation of the performance as soon as practicable after completing the evaluation. The contractor should be allowed at least 30 days to comment on the evaluation. If the parties disagree about the evaluation, refer the evaluation to a level above the contracting office. However, the contracting agency makes the final decision.

Access and Retention

As stated in FAR 42.1503, retain copies of the evaluation, contractor response, and review comments (if any). Mark this information with the legend "Source Selection Information." Only release the evaluation to other Government personnel and the contractor whose performance is being evaluated. Past performance information shall not be retained to provide source selection information for longer than three years after completion of contract performance.

Recording and Sharing Information

The following are some general procedures for recording and sharing of past performance information:

- The agency shall have a system:
  - Evaluations shall be provided to the contractor as soon as practicable after completion of the evaluation.
  - Data is classified "source selection information."
  - Departments and agencies shall share information with other agencies and departments when requested to support future award decisions.

Reporting Negative Performance Information

Report evidence of significant or recurring performance problems, such as:

- Willful failure to perform in accordance with the terms of one or more contracts
- A history of failure to perform or of unsatisfactory performance of one or more contracts
- Violations of the Drug-Free Workplace Act of 1988
- Intentionally affixing a label bearing a "Made in America" inscription to a product sold in or shipped to the United States, when the product was not made in the United States
- Commission of unfair trade practices

Reporting Non-responsibility Determinations

Agencies must report non-responsibility determinations to the debarment official when there is evidence that the contractor cannot be trusted to perform any work.

In particular, the contracting office should report evidence of negative performance collected from other customers of the contractor, a lack of integrity or failure to observe business ethics, and any evidence that the offeror is a front for a debarred or suspended business entity. Include the following in the report:

- Description of the performance problem
- Discussion of mitigating or extenuating circumstances
- An indexed file of related documents
- Any known relationships between the contractor and other entities that have had similar problems
- Analysis of the impact that the contractor's performance problems have had on overall cost, delays in obtaining needed supplies or services, mission accomplishment, and competition
- Provide any additional data requested by the Debarment official in accordance with agency policies and guidelines. Refer to FAR 9.406-3

Summary

Metrics enable you as the Contracting Officer to monitor contractor progress on the current contract, determine customer satisfaction, and provide the required documentation for past contractor performance evaluations. Past performance does not necessarily predict future performance, but it does lower the risk of failure.

Notes

Notes

Notes

Chapter 4 - Contract Commercial and Noncomm Financing

Introduction

When we talk about financing, we are not talking about actually loaning the contractor money but, allowing the contractor to receive funds as the work on the contract progresses, as opposed to waiting until the very end of the contract to receive payment in full.

Government financing shall be provided only to the extent actually needed for prompt and efficient performance, considering the availability of private financing.

Government financing enhances competition as more contractors are encouraged to participate, knowing they will not have to tie up a lot of their resources for long periods of time without payment.

Contract financing shall be administered so as to aid—not impede—the acquisition. At the same time, the Contracting Officer shall avoid any undue risk of monetary loss to the Government through the financing. The contractor's use of the contract financing provided and the contractor's financial status shall be monitored.

INPUT: A contract with commercial financing clause and a request for payment under that clause.

1. Monitor the contractor security provided for Government contract financing.
2. Take appropriate remedial action when the contractor fails to provide required security.
3. Approve a request for commercial financing payment when the request complies with the contract financing clause and other applicable requirements.

Policy on Commercial Financing

It is the responsibility of the contractor to provide all resources needed for performance of the contract. Therefore, for purchases of commercial items, financing of the contract is normally the contractor's responsibility. However, in some markets, the provision of financing by the buyer is a commercial practice.

Because we are encouraged to adopt commercial, or industry, practices when it would be in the best interest of the Government, the Contracting Officer may include appropriate financing terms in contracts for commercial purchases.

There are three types of financing payments available for commercial financing:

- Advance payment
- Interim payment
- Installment payment

Go to FAR 32.202 to find the definitions for Advance Payment, Interim Payment, and Installment Payment.

Security for Government Financing

Commercial financing is available under the following circumstances:

- The contract item financed is a commercial supply or service
- The contract price exceeds the simplified acquisition threshold
- The Contracting Officer determines that it is appropriate or customary in the commercial marketplace to make a financing payment for the item
- Authorizing this form of contract financing is in the best interest of the Government
- Adequate security is obtained
- Prior to any performance of work under the contract, the aggregate of commercial advance payment shall not exceed 15 % of the contract price

Commercial contract financing may be done if the following are true:

1. The contract is awarded on the basis of competitive procedures or, if only one offer is solicited, adequate consideration is obtained (based on the time value of the additional financing to be provided) if the financing is expected to be substantially more advantageous to the offeror than the offeror's normal method of customer financing, and
2. The Contracting Officer obtains concurrence from the payment office concerning liquidation provisions when required by FAR 32.206.

Types of Security

The Government is required to obtain adequate security for Government financing under 10 U.S.C. 2307(f) and 41 U.S.C. 255(f). The contract will specify the type of security the Government will accept, and whether or not the Government is willing to accept more than one form of security. The contractor has to specify the form of security that would be provided prior to the award of the contract as stated in FAR 52.232-29, 30 and 31.

As stated in FAR 32.207, after contract award, the Contracting Officer responsible for approving requests for financing payments shall be responsible for determining that the security continues to be adequate. If the contractor's financial condition is the Government's security, this Contracting Officer also is responsible for monitoring the contractor's financial condition.

FAR 32.202-4 provides the types of security that may be provided by the contractor for approval by the Contracting Officer. When monitoring the security provided by the contractor, the Contracting Officer considers the following:

- If the contractor's financial condition is security for contract financing, the contractor's financial condition will be monitored.
- Assurance that the contractor provides and maintains the type and amount of any other security required by the contract, such as:
  - A paramount lien
  - An irrevocable letter of credit
  - A bond from an acceptable surety
  - A guarantee of repayment from a person or corporation of demonstrated net worth that is connected by significant ownership to the contractor
  - Title to identify assets of adequate worth

FAR 52.232-29 and 30 state, in the event the contractor fails to provide adequate security as required by the contract, the Government will make no financing payments. Upon receipt of adequate security, financing payments shall be made, including all previous payments to which the contractor is entitled. If, at any time during contract performance, additional security is required (i. e., as a result of a deteriorating financial condition), the contractor will be required to provide such additional security as the Contracting Officer determines necessary. If the contractor fails to provide such additional security, the Contracting Officer may:

- Collect or liquidate any security that has been provided
- Suspend further payments to the contractor
- Require the contractor to repay to the Government the amount of unliquidated financing payments as the Contracting Officer deems repayable
- Any combination of the above

Commercial and Noncommercial Financing Payments

The Contracting Officer will approve a request for a commercial financing payment when the request adheres to the contract financing clause and other applicable contract requirements, based on the following:

- The contractor provided adequate security as required by the contract
- The payment request includes all the elements required by FAR 52.232-30
- The amounts are properly calculated and otherwise due
- Prior to performance, advance payments do not total more than 15% of the contract price
- The supplies or services are delivered or performed in accordance with all contract terms and conditions
- The payments will be properly liquidated as required by FAR 32.206

Approval of Payment

The Contracting Officer must consider the following in the approval of the payment:

- The amount to be paid
- All necessary contractual information
- The account(s) to be charged for the payment

Payment Process and Procedures for Noncommercial Contracts

In some fixed-price types of contracts, the Government may agree to provide progress payments to the contractor. A "progress payment" is a form of contract financing made before work or deliverables are accepted. Progress is defined within the context of an affected contract, and such payments are recouped by the Government through the deduction of liquidations, which is determined by an expressed liquidation rate from payments that otherwise would be due to the contractor for completed contract items.

Financing after Award

The Contracting Officer must consider criteria in FAR 32.104 in determining whether to include contract financing through progress payments based on cost in the contract. These payments may be added to a contract based on the contractor's request if it is needed for prompt and efficient contract performance. However, FAR 32.005 adds that new consideration is required for the addition of contract financing after contract award.

In considering whether to provide for progress payments by contract modification, the Contracting Officer will:

1. Determine whether progress payments are needed for prompt and efficient contract performance.
2. Prepare a negotiation position on consideration for adding progress payments considering the following:
   - The contractor may provide new consideration by monetary or nonmonetary means, provided the value is adequate.
   - The fair and reasonable consideration should approximate the amount by which the price would have been less had the contract financing terms been contained in the initial contract. In the absence of definite information, apply the following criteria in evaluating whether the proposed new consideration is adequate:
   - The value to the contractor of the anticipated amount and duration of the contract financing at the imputed financial costs of the equivalent working capital
   - The estimated profit rate to be earned through contract performance
3. Negotiate an acceptable bilateral contract modification.

Approval of Initiation of Progress Payments

Progress payments should be approved as a matter of course for contractors that previous experience or a recent audit review (within the last 12 months) show to be:

- Reliable, competent, and capable of satisfactory performance
- Possessed of an adequate accounting system and controls
- In sound, financial condition

For all other contractors, progress payments must not be approved before determining that:

- Either the Contractor will be capable of liquidating any progress payments, or Government is otherwise protected against loss by additional protective provisions
- The contractor's accounting system and controls are adequate for proper administration of progress payments

Approve or Disapprove Request

When determining whether to approve or disapprove a request, the contracting office should consider:

- When the reliability of the contractor and the adequacy of the contractor's accounting system and controls have been established, rely upon that accounting system and upon the contractor's certification, without requiring audit or review of the request before payment. FAR 32.503-3 and 32.503-4
- Do not routinely ask for audits of progress payment requests. However, ask for a review or audit of the request before approving a payment or otherwise disposing of a request when there is a reason for the ACO to:
  - Question the reliability or accuracy of the contractor's certification
  - Believe that the contract will involve a loss, the ACO should ask for a review or audit of the request before payment is approved or the request is otherwise disposed of
- When there is a reason to doubt the amount of a progress payment request:
  - Only withhold the doubtful amount, subject to later adjustment after review or audit
  - Any clearly proper and due amounts should be paid without awaiting resolution of the differences

Conduct Post-Payment Reviews

While the contractor's accounting system and certification may be relied upon when approving progress payments, post-payment reviews — including audits when considered necessary — must be made periodically, or when considered desirable to determine the validity of progress payments already made and expected to be made.

Post-payment reviews or audits must (as a minimum) include a determination of whether or not:

- The unliquidated progress payments are fairly supported by the value of the work accomplished on the undelivered portion of the contract
- The applicable limitation on progress payments in the Progress Payments clause has been exceeded
- Either the unpaid balance of the contract price will be adequate to cover the anticipated cost of completion, or the Contractor has adequate resources to complete the contract, and there is a reason to doubt the adequacy and reliability of the contractor's accounting system and controls and certification

Under indefinite-delivery contracts, administer progress payments, made under each individual order, as if the order constituted a separate contract unless agency procedures provide otherwise.

Deductions in Payments

The Contracting Officer will liquidate progress payments by deducting them from any payment under this contract (other than advance or progress payments) the unliquidated progress payments, or 80% of the amount invoiced, whichever is less.

The contractor must repay to the Government any amounts required by a retroactive price reduction, after computing liquidations and payments on past invoices at the reduced prices, and adjust the unliquidated progress payments accordingly.

The Government reserves the right to unilaterally change from the ordinary liquidation rate to an alternate rate when deemed appropriate for proper contract financing.

Reduce or Suspend Progress Payment

The Progress Payments clause provides a Government right to reduce or suspend progress payments, increase the liquidation rate, or take other actions under specified conditions. In accordance with FAR 32.503-6, action may be appropriate if:

- The contractor fails to comply with all material requirements of the contract and the failure results from the contractor's fault or negligence.
- Contract performance is endangered by the contractor's unsatisfactory financial condition.

- Inventory allocated to the contract exceeds reasonable requirements.
- The contractor is delinquent in paying the costs of contract performance in the ordinary course of business.
- The fair value of undelivered work is not at least equal to the amount of unliquidated progress payments.
- The sum of the total costs incurred under the contract, plus the estimated costs to complete the contract are likely to exceed the contract price.
- In accordance with FAR 32.503-12, action may be appropriate if unliquidated progress payments exceed the limit in the Progress Payments clause.
- In accordance with FAR 32.503-14, action may be appropriate if the Government's title to inventories under the progress payments clause is compromised by other encumbrances.

Progress Payment Supervision

The Contracting Officer may vary progress payments supervision—by prepayment or periodic review—inversely with the contractor's experience, performance record, reliability, quality of management, and financial strength, and with the adequacy of the contractor's accounting system and controls.

1. Supervision must be of a kind and degree sufficient to provide timely knowledge of the need for, and timely opportunity for, any actions necessary to protect Government interests. Stay informed about the contractor's overall operations and financial condition.
2. Obtain and analyze frequently full information on contract progress, the contractor's other operations, and overall financial condition for contracts with contractors.
3. So far as practicable, all cost problems—particularly those involving indirect costs—that are likely to create disagreements in future administration of the contract should be identified and resolved at the inception of the contract.

Adjust Progress Payment Rate and Issue Modification

Normally, a determination to adjust the progress payment or liquidation rate will be based on a request from the contractor to provide unusual progress payments or reduce the liquidation rate.

Consider such adjustments, when:

- The contractor cash flow is not sufficient to sustain contract performance, even with normal progress and liquidation rates
- The Government is otherwise protected against loss
- The contractor is otherwise capable and competent to perform

Assure that any modification for:

1. A change in the liquidation rate correctly applies the factors at FAR 32.503-10.
2. Use of unusual progress payments:
   - Is approved by the head of the contracting activity
   - Includes adequate consideration from the contractor

Performance-Based Payments

Performance-based payments are fully recoverable, in the same manner as progress payments, in the event of a default. Except when a contract provides for other methods of contract financing, performance-based payments are permitted. For Government accounting purposes, performance-based payments should be treated like progress payments based on cost, and they are not subject to the interest penalty provisions of prompt payment.

These types of payments are the preferred financing method when a Contracting Officer finds them practical, and a contractor agrees to their use. Unless otherwise prescribed by an agency's regulations, performance-based payments may be made either on a whole contract or on a deliverable line-item basis. The Contracting Officer must, at a minimum, identify:

- Performance events or criteria for performance-based payments
- Whether the performance events are severable or cumulative
- Payment amounts
- Any instructions for multiple appropriations
- Method for liquidating performance-based payments
- The minimum interval between performance-based payment requests (i.e., not more frequently than monthly)
- The form and manner in which the contractor must request performance-based payments

Summary

Commercial and non-commercial financial arrangements can assist an otherwise financially healthy contractor in maintaining positive cash flow to meet short-term obligations to suppliers and employees. Financial arrangements should not be considered to keep a financially ailing contractor afloat. The Contracting Officer's responsibility is to use contractor financing to the benefit of the Government in the acquisition of the expected product or service.

Notes

Notes

Notes

Notes

Chapter 5 - Administrative Issues in Labor and Environmental Laws

Introduction

All matters regarding labor relations shall be handled in accordance with agency procedures. Contractual labor clauses provide for the rights and obligations of the parties, specifically the rights of the contractor's employees in terms of wages, benefit packages, and overall welfare.

In some cases, the ACO has little or no responsibility for oversight, but in others, the ACO is fully responsible for monitoring for compliance. Issues regarding labor decisions are handled by the Department of Labor. The Contract Administration Plan should provide a methodology for monitoring the areas that require it. The following clauses are representative of various labor laws and their provisions.

Walsh-Healey Public Contracts Act

The Walsh-Healey Public Contracts Act applies when administering a contract for the manufacture or furnishing of supplies, performed within the U.S., Puerto Rico, or the Virgin Islands, and the contract amount is expected to exceed $15,000, this clause would be incorporated in the contract. FAR 52.222-41

Enforcement of the Provisions of the Walsh-Healey Public Contracts Act

The clause requires that contractor employees be paid minimum wage rates based on Department of Labor (DOL) wage determinations. There are exceptions for certain categories of employees, such as apprentices. The Contracting Officer is not responsible for the enforcement of this law. However, if the Contracting Officer becomes aware of violations in the course of contract administration they shall, in accordance with agency procedures, notify the appropriate regional office of the DOL, Wage, and Hour Division. *common in CDC.*

Service Contract Act of 1965, As Amended

The Service Contract Act of 1965 applies when administering a service contract in the U.S. that has a dollar value of over $2,500. The FAR clause, 52.222-41 Service Contract of 1965, As Amended, will have to be included in the solicitation and the contract. The clause requires that contractor employees are paid at least minimum wage and fringe benefits, and are paid at least twice a month in accordance with the DOL wage rates in the contract. The DOL has the responsibility of developing and updating the wage rates. This is completed by region, on an annual basis. *does not apply for overseas contract.*

Enforcement of the Service Contract Act

Part of the requirement of administering a service contract is to incorporate updated wage determinations annually. This is a key role the Contracting Officer plays in ensuring the contractor adheres to the current wage rates for the contractor's employees. A change in wage determinations may create a requirement for an equitable adjustment. The Contracting Officer is not responsible for enforcing the Service Contract Act as the DOL enforces these requirements.

Fair Labor Standards Act

The Fair Labor Standards Act applies to service contracts with a value over $2,500 if there is no predecessor contractor that had a collective bargaining agreement. The wage determination—issued under the Service Contract Act—requires a current wage determination on the anniversary date of a multiple-year contract or the beginning of each renewal option period. FAR 52.222-43

The contractor shall notify the Contracting Officer of any increase claimed under this law within 30 days after receiving a new wage determination.

Enforcement of the Fair Labor Standards Act

The DOL is responsible for enforcement of this labor law. The labor standards for contraction contracts cover laborers and mechanics and include requirements for contracts in excess of $2,000 for contraction, alteration, or repair performed in the U.S. Included in this group are Davis Bacon, Copeland Act, and the Contract Work Hours and Safety Standards Act. The DOL is responsible for updating regional wage rates, and the contractor is required to keep them posted where all employees have access to them.

Davis-Bacon Act

The Davis-Bacon Act labor standard requires that the laborers and mechanics on a construction contract valued over $2,000 be paid weekly. The clause requires that any laborer or mechanic employed directly upon the site of the work shall receive at least the prevailing wage rates as determined by the Secretary of Labor. FAR 52.222-6

Contract Work Hours and Safety Standards Act: Overtime Compensation

The Contract Work Hours and Safety Standards Act also applies to laborers and mechanics, and provides for overtime pay for any hours over the 40 work-hours per week, at the rate of one and one-half their basic rate of pay. FAR 52.222-4

Contracting agencies are responsible for ensuring the full and impartial enforcement of labor standards in the administration of construction contracts.

The Contracting Officer is required to monitor adherence to these labor laws by performing payroll reviews, on-site inspections, and conducting employee interviews to determine compliance by the contractor and subcontractors and prompt initiation of corrective action when required. If violations are found, a thorough investigation is conducted.

If the contractor does not make restitution, the Contracting Officer shall complete a Contracting Officer's Report. If the report verifies the violation, a detailed enforcement report shall be submitted to the Administrator of the Wage and Hour Division within 60 days after completion of the Contracting Officer's investigation. This action may include termination of the contract by the Contracting Officer.

Enforcement of Labor Laws

In addition to the clauses for the enforcement of labor laws, there also are a number of other clauses required for the enforcement of related laws. Similar to the labor laws, the contract professional may or may not be responsible for the enforcement, but must know:

- What is in the contract
- The responsibilities of the contractor
- Who is responsible for the administration of the specific clause

Learner Reference

The following list presents some miscellaneous terms and conditions, including environmental issues, describing the purpose and associated administrative responsibilities.

FAR 52.204-2 Security Requirements

Use – This clause applies to the contracts in which the contractor will have access to classified documentation.

Admin – Agency security procedures will provide oversight to ensure the contractor follows required guidelines and submits reports. The CO will ensure the contractor follows through with security documentation.

FAR 52.223-3 Hazardous Material Identification and Material Safety Data

Use – In contracts requiring the delivery of hazardous materials.

Admin – Contractor is required to keep the Material Safety Data Sheet, in accordance with Federal Standard No. 313, which lists updated hazardous material. Oversight is provided by Occupational Safety Health Agency (OSHA), and the CO should report suspected violations to OSHA.

FAR 52.223-6 Drug-Free Workplace

Use – Any dollar value to an individual, otherwise any contract over the simplified acquisition threshold performed in the U.S., except for the acquisition of commercial items (FAR 23.501).

Admin – Failure to comply with the requirements of this clause may make it necessary for the CO to suspend payments, terminate the contract for default, and authorize suspension or debarment.

FAR 52.228-5 Insurance—Work on a Government Installation

Use – Fixed Price contracts, over the simplified acquisition threshold performed on Government installations in the U.S.

Admin – Prior to performance beginning the contractor is required to provide notification to the CO that required insurance has been obtained. The CO must monitor its receipt and annual renewals.

FAR 52.237-2 Protection of Government Buildings, Equipment, and Vegetation

Use – Services to be performed on Government installations, no construction.

Admin – The CO enforces the requirement to perform service without damaging items covered by the clause. The CO can deduct the cost if the contractor fails to replace or make repairs.

Summary

The labor, environmental, and other miscellaneous terms and conditions in the contract must be addressed, and the contract administrator must know exactly whom the responsible parties are based on the clauses in the contract. In many cases, the contractor would be required to comply with provisions of other Federal statutes whether or not they stated specifically in the contract. A prime example is environmental law and regulations that may be supplemented with state and local requirements. As a rule of thumb, the CO should monitor without specific oversight. The caution is that the CO does not want to give the appearance of validating a contractor's action, which may or may not be in compliance with other legal statutes.

Notes

Notes

Notes

Notes

Chapter 6 - Commercial and Non-Commercial Remedies

Introduction

Government contract remedies are forms of relief that can be pursued for contractor non-performance or non-compliance with the contract's terms and conditions. These forms of relief are provided by contract clauses or from the basic rights of Government and commercial contract law.

Government Policy

In seeking contract remedies, Government policy requires its agents to:

- Document and verify the sufficiency of evidence for the remedy sought
- Notify the contractor of the Government's intention to seek relief
- Obtain contractor feedback on a proposed Government action

Monitoring identifies or permits the surfacing of performance failures or other breaches of contract situations, such as anticipated or actual late delivery, failure to control costs adequately, and unsatisfactory performance.

When performance failures or other breach-of-contract situations arise, the CO must conduct an investigation to determine whether the contractor, the Government, or both have failed to comply with the contract requirements. The Government should ascertain that the language of the contract is free from ambiguities, and its terms and conditions are clear and free from misinterpretation.

The CO also should consider if the current contractor's representatives were involved in the negotiation of the contract (if applicable). The price negotiation memorandum can be reviewed to confirm what transpired during the negotiations, what parties represented the contractor, and what, if any, techniques were employed by the contractor, (i.e., was the proposal "gold plated?") or where concessions made by the contractor just to get the award of the contract. Verification by the CO that the Government has carried out its promises and responsibilities will be documented. For example:

- Furnishing of suitable Government property at the specified time and place, as required by Government-furnished property contract clauses
- Implied duty not to hinder performance, as required by inspection contract clauses
- Implied duty to disclose information vital for offer preparation or contract performance, adherence to the Freedom of Information Act by acquisition personnel
- Implied duty to provide factually correct information
- Implied warranty of specifications

The CO will meet with members of the acquisition team to analyze potential defenses to allegations that the:

- Contractor failed to comply with contract requirements, such as:
- Impracticability of performance
    - o Does the contractor's documentation support that, in the event, the contractor followed the specification, the end result of the contract requirement would be impossible to meet?
    - o Mutual mistakes
- Unconscionable requirements
- Were the requirements unreasonable? If it is a commercial acquisition, is the requirement not considered standard practice? And if so, was the requirement an issue discussed prior to award?
- The government failed to comply with contract requirements, such as:
    - o Disclaimers during negotiations
    - o The Sovereign Acts Doctrine, which bars claims against the Government for actions that it takes in its sovereign capacity. A sovereign act possesses three characteristics:
        1. The act must be of general applicability and public in nature
        2. The contracting agency must not be the motivating force behind the actions
        3. Congress must not have expressly waived sovereign immunity

Remedies

The CO must recognize the remedy or remedies that best match the problem and the extent (if any) to which the Government is at fault.

Generally, the following remedies will be considered:

- Cure notice and the possibility of contract termination for cause
- Rejection of supplies or services before or after acceptance and possible termination for cause
- Remedies under a warranty clause (if incorporated as an addendum to FAR 52.212-4)
- Remedies under implied warranties (e.g., the warranty of merchantability or the warranty of fitness for a particular purpose)
- Termination for convenience or cause
- Any other remedies provided in the specific clause that was breached

Non-conforming Supply or Service

Alternatively, it may be in the Government's best interest to accept a supply or service that is non-conforming with additional contractor consideration (FAR 46.407). However, before accepting a non-conforming supply, coordinate with the end-user to ensure it is acceptable.

Withholding or Reducing Payment

The Government may withhold or reduce payment, as provided in the contract.
- No payment is due under the:
    - Terms for Financing Purchases of Commercial items clause (FAR 52.232-29) when supplies or services will not be delivered or performed in accordance with the contract
    - Installment Payment for Commercial Items clause (FAR 52.232-30) when supplies or services will not be delivered or performed according to contract
- Reduced payment may be taken under:
    - FAR 52.232-1 and FAR 32.006 for delivered and accepted supplies or services to reflect any downward adjustment in the price agreed to by the contractor and called out in the contract

Appropriate Commercial Remedies

The following table reflects situations that may arise during contract performance, a choice of possible commercial contract remedies for that problem, and the applicable references.

Selecting a Commercial Remedy		
Problem	**Remedy**	**Reference(s)**
Late Delivery.	Reschedule the delivery date in exchange for consideration when: 1. There is a reasonable probability of delivery by the new date, and 2. The requiring activity can live with the new date.	N/A
When the CO has determined that the deliverable has been or will be delivered late and that the delay is inexcusable.	Reduce or suspend commercial finance payments. Appropriate when: 1. Commercial finance payments are being made, and 2. Contract performance is endangered by the contractor's failure to make progress.	FAR 52.232-29 FAR 52.232-30

Accept late delivery and impose liquidated damages. Appropriate when: 1. The contract provides for liquidated damages, and 2. There is a reasonable probability of delivery by a date that the requiring activity can tolerate.	Accept late delivery and impose liquidated damages. Appropriate when: 1. The contract provides for liquidated damages, and 2. There is a reasonable probability of delivery by a date that the requiring activity can tolerate.	FAR 52.212-4
	Send a cure notice (10 days or more prior to the contract's delivery date) or a termination notice (immediately upon expiration of the delivery period) when there is little probability of delivery by a date that the requiring activity can tolerate and/or the contractor has not offered adequate consideration	FAR 52.212-4 FAR 49.607 FAR 12.403
The deliverable has been accepted but does not conform to the contract's requirements.	Reject work after acceptance if the Government reports the defect to the contractor within a reasonable time after the defect was discovered or should have been discovered, and before substantial change occurs in the condition of the item unless the change is due to the defect in the item.	FAR 52.212-4
	Invoke an express warranty if a warranty clause has been incorporated by an addendum.	FAR 52.212-4 FAR 12.404
	Invoke an implied warranty if an implied warranty applies.	FAR 52.212-4 FAR 12.404
Accept late delivery and impose liquidated damages. Appropriate when: 1. The contract provides for liquidated damages, and 2. There is a reasonable probability of delivery by a date that the requiring activity can tolerate.	Accept late delivery and impose liquidated damages. Appropriate when: 1. The contract provides for liquidated damages, and 2. There is a reasonable probability of delivery by a date that the requiring activity can tolerate.	FAR 52.212-4
	Send a cure notice (10 days or more prior	FAR 52.212-

	to the contract's delivery date) or a termination notice (immediately upon expiration of the delivery period) when there is little probability of delivery by a date that the requiring activity can tolerate and/or the contractor has not offered adequate consideration	4 FAR 49.607 FAR 12.403
The deliverable has been accepted but does not conform to the contract's requirements.	Reject work after acceptance if the Government reports the defect to the contractor within a reasonable time after the defect was discovered or should have been discovered, and before substantial change occurs in the condition of the item unless the change is due to the defect in the item.	FAR 52.212-4
	Invoke an express warranty if a warranty clause has been incorporated by an addendum.	FAR 52.212-4 FAR 12.404
	Invoke an implied warranty if an implied warranty applies.	FAR 52.212-4 FAR 12.404

Appropriate Non-Commercial Remedies

The following chart reflects situations that may arise during contract performance, a choice of possible non-commercial remedies, and the applicable references.

Available Remedies Under Non-Commercial Contracts		
Problem	**Remedy**	**Reference(s)**
Time of delivery or performance is delinquent.	Assess the liquidated damages in accordance with the contract and make the appropriate monetary reductions.	FAR 52.211-11, Liquidated Damages

Variation in quantity is detected.	Normal business practice does not require exact quantity (within established tolerance).	FAR 52.211-16, Variance in Quantity
The contractor has shipped more than required by the contract.	The government would otherwise suffer the expense of shipping excess quantity (<$250 or >$250) back to the contractor.	FAR 52.211-17, Delivery of Excess Quantities
The contractor is requiring laborers/mechanics to work in excess of 40 hours and not compensating them at a rate of at least one and one-half times their normal rate.	Contract workers are not being paid required rate after 40 hours per week. (DOL is responsible for enforcement).	FAR 52.222-4, Contract Work Hours and Safety Standards Act
The contractor has discriminated against one or more of its workers because of race, color, religion, sex, or national origin.	Government shall terminate for default, should the contractor fail to correct the situation. (The Office of Federal Contract Compliance Programs determines non-compliance.)	FAR 52.222-26, Equal Opportunity
The contractor's employees are compensated less than the Secretary of Labor's required minimum wage and benefits	Withhold monies due the contractor should non-compliance continue.	FAR 52.222-41, Service Contract Act
The contractor is not adequately conducting inspections of supplies or services, nor is the contractor keeping accurate records, or the contractor is failing to make such inspection records available to Government representatives, or fails to allow Government inspection of the same.	Withhold monies due the contractor should non-compliance continue, **and/or** Government chooses to terminate for default, should the contractor fail to correct the situation.	Inspection and acceptance clauses: FAR 52.246-2, Supplies, Fixed-Price FAR 52.246-3, Supplies, Cost Reimbursement FAR 52.246-4, Services, Fixed-Price FAR 52.246-5, Services, Cost Reimbursement FAR 52.246-6, Time and Material, and Labor Hour

		FAR 52.246-7, Research and Development, Fixed-Price FAR 52.246-8, Research and Development, Cost Reimbursement
Supplies and/or services are not of the quality specified and do not conform in all respects with contract requirements, including specifications, drawings, preservation, packaging, packing, marking requirements, and physical item identification (part number), or are not of the required quantity according to the certificate of conformance.	Government shall reject defective supplies or services within a reasonable time after delivery, **and** withhold monies due to the contractor should non-compliance continue, **and/or** the Government may choose to terminate for default, should the contractor fail to correct the situation.	Certificate of Conformance.
The supplies or service fail to perform as stated in the contract within the warranty period.	The Contracting Officer shall require the contractor to correct or re-perform services or replace supplies as appropriate, according to the contract warranty, **and** withhold monies due the contractor should non-compliance continue.	Warranty Clauses: FAR 52.246-17, Supplies of a Non-complex Nature FAR 52.246-18, Supplies of a Complex Nature FAR 52.246-19, Systems and Equipment FAR 52.246-20, Warranty of Services
Government property is damaged while in the possession of the contractor.	The extent of contractor's liability will be either any loss, damage, or destruction; or only loss, damage or destruction due to lack of good faith or willful misconduct on the part of managerial personnel.	Limitation of Liability: High-Value Items Services

The contractor has failed to: 1. Deliver the supplies or to perform the services within the time specified in the contract; or 2. Make progress so as to endanger performance of the contract; or 3. Perform any other provisions of the contract.	Government shall terminate for default (in whole or in part), should the contractor fail to correct the situation, **and** pay contract price for completed supplies delivered or service performed & accepted, **and** the contractor will be found liable for any excess costs to complete the performance of the contract, **and** the Government shall require the contractor to transfer title and deliver to the Government any completed or partially completed work.	Default Clauses: FAR 52.249-8, Supply and Service, Fixed-Price FAR 52.249-9, Research and Development, Fixed-Price FAR 52.249-10, Construction, Fixed-Price
The contractor has failed to establish clear evidence that the delivery of required items had latent defects was unknown to the contractor.	The government may replace or correct the items/service, **and** charge the cost to the contractor, **or** negotiated an equitable adjustment in contract price, **or** terminate the contract for default, **and/or** initiate debarment action.	Default clauses: FAR 52.249-8, Supply and Service, Fixed-Price FAR 52.249-9, Research and Development, Fixed-Price FAR 52.249-10, Construction, Fixed-Price FAR 9.406

Summary

Commercial and non-commercial remedies to contractor non-performance or non-compliance protect the interests of the Government.

Your first objectives as a CO should be to seek always fulfillment of the contract to get the product or service to the customer. You should seek to resolve problems. Use the tools available to you and communicate with the contractor and customer.

Notes

Notes

Notes

Notes

Chapter 7 - Paying the Invoice

Introduction

It is the Government's intention to pay its obligations to contractors for products or services received on time. For many contractors, particularly small business contractors, prompt payment is necessary to maintain day-to-day positive cash flow. However, payment must be submitted, authorized, and documented properly to protect the Government's financial interest.

Elements of a Proper Invoice

As stated in FAR 32.904, the due date for making an invoice payment by the designated payment office shall be the 30th day after the designated billing office has received a proper invoice from the contractor. FAR 32.905 identifies the criteria for what constitutes a proper invoice. When using fast payment procedures, the criteria for a proper invoice are found in FAR 52.213-1. The contracting office is responsible for processing invoices meeting FAR and Prompt Payment Act requirements as identified in FAR 32.9.

Procedures to Determine the Amount to Be Paid to the Contractor

The documents and determinations that affect the amount to be paid must be obtained and reviewed to verify acceptance of supplies and/or services. The following are examples of such documents and determinations:

- Inspection or receiving report forms or commercial shipping documents and packing lists
- Documentation on the application of remedies, such as liquidated damages or rejection of work
- Determinations on billing rates, final indirect cost rates, and on the allowability of invoiced costs
- Reports on contractor indebtedness
- Adjustments to liquidation rates or reductions in commercial financing, advance, progress, or performance-based payments
- Interim or final adjustments to the contract price
- Contract modifications
- Contracting Officer's final decision on a claim
- Termination settlements

The documentation identifies items and the related amount that must be deducted or withheld from the invoice payment. Those items identified and the amounts deducted must be examined to determine that the deductions were taken in accordance with the contract terms and conditions.

Learner Reference

Review the following table for deductions that may be taken from invoice amounts.

WHEN	DEDUCT	IAW FAR
Administering fixed-price contracts.	Invoiced items that have not been delivered and accepted. Invoiced prices that exceed the contract price for the supplies or services. Invoiced partial payments when the amount due on the deliverables is less than $1,000 or 50% of contract price.	52.232-1 and 52.232-2
	Invoiced amounts for "extras."	52.232-11
	Discounts for early payment.	52.232-25
	State and local taxes, by furnishing the contractor with evidence of any exemption from such taxes.	52.229-1
	After-relieved Federal or foreign taxes. **	52.229-3 to 52.229-7
	The amount of any Federal excise tax or duty (except social security or other employment taxes) that the contractor is required to pay or bear, or does not obtain a refund of, through the contractor's fault, negligence or failure to follow the Contracting Officer's instructions.	
Billed for transportation costs	Improperly supported reimbursement for transportation charges.	52.247-1
Modifying the contract	Unilateral or bilateral downward adjustments to the contract price (including adjustments that result from the resolution of performance problems).	52.243-1 to 52.243-7, and 52.248-1.
Implementing special contract remedies	Liquidated damages, such as those under the: Liquidated Damages – Supplies, Services, or Research and Development clause (FAR 52.211-11). Liquidated Damages – Small Business Subcontracting Plan clause (FAR 52.219-16); or Contract Work Hours and Safety Standards Act-Overtime Compensation (FAR 52.222-4).	52.211-11, 52.219-16, and 52.222-4
Collecting contractor debts.	Setoffs for the collection of contractor debts.	32.6
Progress payments are being made.	From invoiced prices, amounts necessary to liquidate prior progress payments (as calculated under the terms of the Progress Payments clause.) Unallowable costs invoiced on the SF 1443, Contractor's	52.232-16

	Request for Progress Payment. Costs invoiced on the SF 1443, Contractor's Request for Progress Payments, when a decision has been made to suspend or reduce progress payments.	
Administering a cost reimbursement contract	Retainages, such as: 15% of fee up to $100,000 that may be withheld under FAR 52.216-8 for cost-plus-fixed-fee contracts or FAR 52.216-10 for cost-plus-incentive-fee contracts. 1% of total estimated cost up to $100,000 under FAR 52.216-11 for cost contracts with no fee. Payment on the basis of a lower fee under cost-plus-incentive-fee contracts, when the contractor is not likely to achieve the target. Unallowable costs. Over-billed indirect costs, given billing rates or final indirect cost rates for the period. Costs in excess of the limitation of costs or limitation of funds in cost-reimbursement contracts. Any tax or duty of a foreign Government from which the U.S. Government is exempt by agreement with the foreign government.	52.216-7, 52.216-8 52.216-10, and 52.216-11 52.229-8 or 52.229-9
Administering a fixed-price incentive contract	The amount by which invoiced prices exceed current billing prices (e.g., when billing prices are reduced). The amount by which billing prices exceed the final prices for deliverables.	52.216-16 and 52.216-17
Administering a time-and-materials or labor-hour contract.	Any amount in excess of the ceiling price. A retainage of 5% of the amount due up to $50,000 until execution and delivery of the contractor's release. Overpayments or improper amounts for materials or subcontracts.	52.232-7
Administering a letter contract	Invoiced amounts in excess of the limitation of reimbursement or reimbursement rates.	52.216-26
Royalties are being paid. **	Royalties in excess of the amount owed by the Government.	52.227-9
Terminating a contract.	Invoiced amounts that are greater than the amount authorized for partial payment or final payment of the termination settlement. Re-procurement costs and costs for any other damages suffered by the Government.	49.112, 49.402-6, and 49.402-7(b).

** Do not pay the invoiced amount for a royalty when:

> The Government has a royalty-free license which covers that royalty.
> Billed at a rate in excess of the rate for which the Government is licensed.
> The royalties in whole or in part otherwise constitute an improper charge.

Request for Payment

The Government will determine the amount to be paid on the contractor's request for payment. This will be accomplished by performing and verifying the mathematical computations based on the verification of internal reports and determinations and the terms and conditions of the contract.

The Contracting Officer will contact the contractor to discuss any differences between the amount of the submitted invoice and the amount that the Government proposes to pay. During the discussion, the Government will:

- Accurately present all factual data that justifies the difference between the invoiced amount and the amount that the Government proposed to pay
- Provide contractor representatives an opportunity to present their position
- Ensure that the contractor's management is aware of any continuing invoicing problems

After the discussion with the contractor, the Contracting Officer determines the amount to pay on the contractor's request. The determination would have taken into account the following alternatives:

Pay in full

- Pay in part, after written notice to the contractor specifying the deductions and/or withholdings
- Reject the invoice and return it to the contractor for correction and resubmission, specifying the reason
- If the invoice is returned to the contractor for correction, the Contracting Officer must adhere to the conditions stated in FAR 32.907 to avoid payment of a late payment and any applicable interest

As stated in FAR 32.907, the contractor is to be notified of deductions or withholdings from the amount invoiced within 30 days after the designated billing office has received a proper invoice from the contractor, or within 30 days after Government acceptance, whichever is later (assuming no disagreement over quantity, quality, or contractor compliance with contract requirements).

The approved invoice is submitted to the Finance Office in a timely manner (within the meaning of the Prompt Payment Act), and within the time standards agreed upon between the Contracting Officer and the certifying finance officer.

Policies and Procedures for Setoffs

Generally, when a contractor owes the Government money, i.e., past-due taxes, overpayments, liquidated damages, etc., we can deduct that amount from other payments due to the contractor. The liability doesn't have to result from this contract for us to be able to recoup the money owed from this contract. This process is called a setoff.

You may include in your contract a no-setoff commitment that would prevent the Government from reducing the payments that will be made to the financial institution, the assignee, because the contractor owes us money. When an assigned contract does not include a no-setoff commitment, the Government may reduce the payments to the financial institution. The use of a no-setoff provision may be appropriate:

- To facilitate the national defense
- In the event of a national emergency or natural disaster
- When the use of the no-setoff provision may facilitate private financing of contract performance

However, if the contractor is significantly indebted to the Government, you should consider whether the inclusion of the no-setoff commitment in a particular contract is in the best interests of the Government. In such an event, you should consult with the Government officer(s) responsible for collecting the debt(s) owed by the contractor. For DoD, the general policy is to include a no-setoff provision in all contracts unless you make the determination that not including it is in the Government's best interest. Even if your contract includes a no-setoff provision, you may be able to reduce contract payments because of contractor indebtedness to the Government when the financial institution isn't processing or hasn't processed an actual loan to the contractor or when the amount due on the contract exceeds the amount of any loans subject to the assignment.

Summary

In most cases, your contract payment processing will become routine. Miscommunication can cause you problems, especially if the contractor doesn't understand what deductions or adjustments will be made to the payment. Again, as in most contract administration actions, document your work.

www.acquisition.gov
change details:
FAR part 31/32

Notes

Notes

Notes

Chapter 8 - Types of Modifications

Introduction

A contract modification is any written change in terms of a contract. The Contracting Officer is the only person who has the authority to change the terms of the contract by processing a modification to a Government contract. There are two types of modifications: bilateral and unilateral.

- Unilateral modifications are modifications signed only by the Government's Contracting Officer.
- Bilateral modifications, also known as supplemental agreements, are modifications that are signed by both contracting parties: the Contracting Officer and the contractor.

Unilateral modifications

Unilateral modifications are used to:

- Make administrative changes (i.e., correct a typo in the accounting line or change the address of the payment office)
- Issue change orders
- Make changes authorized by other contract clauses (e.g., Options clause, FAR 52.217-7, and Suspension of Work clause, FAR 52.242-14
- Issue termination notices

You would elect to process a unilateral modification when the:

- Change has no substantive effect on the contractor or the Government
- Change can be made unilaterally under a specific contract term
- Contractor's agreement is not required

Example: You are administering a construction contract. The Contracting Officer's Representative (COR) informs you that the Government and the contractor are conflicted over the interpretation of one of the architectural elements as displayed in the contract drawings. The COR relates that no further work can be performed on the contract until the dispute is resolved. As the Contracting Officer, you issue a unilateral modification, ordering the contractor to suspend work on the contract, under the authority of contract clause 52.242-14 Suspension of Work.

Example of Unilateral Modifications: Change orders

One of the most widely recognized uses of a unilateral modification is as a change order. A change order is a signed modification from the Contracting Officer that directs the contractor to make a change that the "Changes" clause authorizes without the contractor's consent. There are several changes clauses in the FAR:

- 52.243-1 Changes – Fixed Price
- 52.243-2 Changes – Cost-Reimbursement
- 52.243-3 Changes – Time-and-Materials or Labor-Hours
- 52.243-4 Changes
- 52.243-5 Changes and Changed Conditions
- 52.212-4 Contract Terms and Conditions – Commercial Items

For supplemental regulatory information about contract changes, read FAR 43.2.

The Contracting Officer unilaterally invokes the clause for contract changes that are specifically authorized under the applicable changes clause. Under the Changes clauses, the contractor has the right to request an equitable adjustment for the directed change as described below under bilateral modifications.

Definition of Definitization

There are times when all the details of the work to be done are not known, but we need the work, or change, to start immediately. As soon as we can, we have to make definite what was previously unknown. Definitization means we are defining, or making definite, exactly what the contract terms and conditions are: specifications, price, and other terms as necessary.

Example of when a Unilateral Mod leads to a Bilateral Modification

The definitization of a contract change is issued as a supplemental agreement to the contract, which is agreed to and signed by both parties. The supplemental agreement for the definitization is, therefore, a bilateral modification.

Bilateral modifications

Bilateral modifications are used to:

- Make negotiated equitable adjustments—contract modifications that are fair and reasonable to both contracting parties—to the contract resulting from the issuance of a change order
- Definitize—supplemental agreement reflecting the resulting equitable adjustment in contract terms, prices or costs—letter contracts
- Reflect other agreements of the contracting parties modifying the terms of contracts

Example: You are administering a firm-fixed-price construction contract. The Contracting Officer's Representative (COR) informs you that the customer wants the building materials changed from brick to sandstone block. You verify that the customer has the additional funds to cover the difference in materials cost. Under the authority of clause 52.243-2, Changes – Fixed Price, you issue a unilateral modification to the contract instructing the contractor to change the type of materials.

This same clause gives the contractor the right to request an equitable adjustment in the contract price, to fairly reimburse him for the increased cost of the sandstone block. In accordance with the clause, the contractor has 30 days to submit his request for equitable adjustment and to submit documentation to support his new price. Once you and the contractor have agreed on the increased price of the contract due to the directed contract change, you then issue a bilateral modification (supplemental agreement) to definitize the cost of the change.

It is important to know that there are two types of modifications.

Unilateral modifications can be used to change the payment office address, correct a typo in the accounting line, or terminate a contract. These are examples of when only the Contracting Officer has to sign because we do not need the contractor's concurrence on these changes. Bilateral modifications do require that we get an agreement with the contractor before we change the contract.

General Scope of the Contract

In order to make a determination as to whether a contract modification is within the general scope of the contract, a Contracting Officer should consider:

- What was reasonably within the mindset of the parties at the time the contract was signed? This would be evidenced by documentation of negotiations, an acquisition plan, and most importantly, the contract document itself.
- The function of the end item
- Nature and purpose of the contract

Notes

Notes

Notes

Chapter 9 - Steps for Processing a Modification

Introduction

Whatever the basis for a modification, the authority to process the modification is always restricted to situations in which the Government receives adequate value in exchange for an agreement to modify a contract, what we in contracting call consideration. In some instances, adequate consideration will reflect a factor tradeoff resulting in no increase or decrease in price, as in a no-cost contract modification.

Modifications of letter contracts (which are written preliminary contractual instruments that authorize the contractor to begin work immediately, but for which the cost or price and other contract terms and applicable clauses have yet to be determined) are subject to the same policies and procedures as modifications of definitive contracts. Definitive contracts are bilateral contracts with agreed-upon terms, conditions, and costs or prices.

To process a modification, certain steps must be followed for both a commercial or non-commercial contract. A contract modification can be initiated by either party: the contractor or the Government. Either way, the contracting professional will need to evaluate the proposed contract change as depicted in the chart below under Step 1.

Steps for Processing a Modification
1a. Evaluate the contractor's request for proposed contract change
1b. Evaluate the Government's request for proposed contract change
2. Determine whether to make a modification to the contract
3. Determine whether to use a unilateral or bilateral modification
4a. Modify the contract using a unilateral modification
4b. Modify the contract using a bilateral modification
5. Document the contract file and distribute the modification

1a. Evaluate the contractor's request for proposed contract change

A contractor may request a contract modification when the reason for a modification falls into one of the following three categories:

- Beyond the contractor's control, as in:
  - An excusable delay
  - A settlement for termination for convenience of the Government
  - A stop-work order
- Due to action by the contractor, as in:
  - A company name change,
  - The submission of value engineering change proposal
  - A consideration offered for other than an excusable delay
- Required by the contract, as in:
  - An economic price adjustment
  - A Department of Labor wage rate increase when exercising an option on a service contract
  - A price redetermination

Because the contractor is initiating the request and is familiar with the details of the proposed change, the contractor is required to provide all applicable supporting documentation (quotes, invoices, payroll records, legal documents, accounting data, etc.) for the proposed contract change.

Because the contract has been awarded, the Government and the contractor are now in a sole-source environment. The negotiations for an equitable adjustment must be handled as any other sole source negotiations would be approached. If the sum total of the contract, any other modifications with monetary adjustments and the current modification exceed any threshold for a Justification and Approval (J&A), the J&A will be written and included in the contract.

1b. Evaluate the Government's request for proposed contract change

At any time after award, the Government may need to make changes to the requirements covered by the contract. Examples of Government proposed changes include:

- Customer's fund cite or accounting data changes
- Delivery or inspection location changes
- Confirmation of a constructive change

A constructive change is work performed by the contractor that is not required by the contract (without a formal change order), that in the contractor's perspective, was informally ordered by the Government or was caused by the Government's action or inaction.

Example: You, the Contracting Officer, are administering a firm-fixed-price construction contract. You receive an invoice from the contractor for overtime work he performed on the weekend. After review of the contract, you determine that overtime premium pay is NOT provided for in the contract price. The contractor reveals to you that the base commander instructed him to accelerate completion of the project by 15 days, and the only way he could accomplish this request is through overtime work.

There was no contract modification issued accelerating delivery on this contract. The contractor incorrectly assumed that the base commander had the authority to make changes to the contract. This is an example of a constructive change.

Once you verify with the base commander that he did indeed accelerate performance, you will need to confirm the constructive change, negotiate an equitable adjustment, obtain more funds from the customer, and issue a supplemental agreement through the execution of a bilateral modification.

2. Determine whether to make a modification to the contract

The Contracting Officer has to determine whether or not a modification is in order. A modification should not be issued if:

- What would be modified is already covered by the contract
- Technical changes cannot be supported to the requiring activity's satisfaction
- Changes to non-technical business terms and conditions are unacceptable
- Additional funds are not available to fund the modification

3. Determine whether to use a unilateral or bilateral modification

As previously discussed, unilateral modifications may be used for:

- Administrative changes
- Issuing change orders under the changes clause
- Making unilateral changes authorized by clauses other than the changes clause
- The issuing of termination notices

Most administrative changes correct non-substantive errors—which do not affect the terms, conditions, or price—in the original contract document.

Bilateral modifications are necessary when definitizing change orders and letter contracts, and to reflect other agreements of the contracting parties that alter the terms of the contract (substantive changes). As a general rule, if the modification affects price, delivery, quantity, or quality, the modification would be issued bilaterally.

4a. Modify the contract using a unilateral modification

When it is determined that a unilateral modification is to be issued—you, the contracting professional—prepare the documentation and the Contracting Officer signs the modification.

4b. Modify the contract using a bilateral modification

When a determination has been made to issue a bilateral modification, you shall first obtain a proposal and supporting documentation for the proposal or offer from the contractor.

With the assistance of other members of the Government acquisition team, you will evaluate the contractor's proposal; you may have to conduct fact-finding and establish a pre-negotiation position on any equitable adjustment or other consideration due either the contractor or the Government as a result of the contract change.

Negotiations then will be held with the contractor to reach agreement on all contract elements affected by the modification. For example, cost changes and/or delivery impacts.

Then, you will prepare the modification documentation and forward it to the contractor for signature. The signs the modification first, and the Contracting Officer signs last. Because the Contracting Officer's signature makes the contract legally binding on the Government, the contractor needs to sign first.

5. Document the contract file and distribute the modification

The contract file will be documented to reflect the basis for decisions made by the contracting professional during the modification process to include the original of the modification document.

To avoid subsequent controversies that may result from a supplemental agreement containing an equitable adjustment as the result of a change order, you should include in the supplemental agreement, a statement of release, similar to the following:

Contractor's Statement of Release

In consideration of the modification(s) agreed to herein as complete equitable adjustments for the Contractor's _____ (describe)_____ "proposal(s) for adjustment," the Contractor hereby releases the Government from any and all liability under this contract for further equitable adjustments attributable to such facts or circumstances giving rise to the "proposal(s) for adjustment" (except for _____).

Distribution of the modification should include all the parties on the contract distribution list. Additional parties for modification distribution may be added to the distribution list because of their participation in the modification analysis and negotiations or who need to know the results.

SF 30 – When it SHALL be used

The Standard Form 30 (SF 30), Amendment of Solicitation/Modification of Contract, shall be used for (except for actions under FAR Part 15, Contracting by Negotiation):

- Any amendment to a solicitation
- Any unilateral contract modification issued under a contract clause, including the Changes Clause, that authorizes a modification without the consent of the contractor
- Administrative contract changes
- Supplemental agreements
- Removal, reinstatement, or addition of funds to a contract

SF 30 – When it MAY be used

The SF 30 may also be used for:

- Actions processed under FAR Part 15, Contracting By Negotiation
- Termination notices
- Purchase order modifications as specified in FAR Part 13, Simplified Acquisition Procedures

Optional Form 336

The Optional Form 336 (OF 336), Continuation Sheet, or a blank sheet of paper, may be used as a continuation sheet for a contract modification.

Summary

In this chapter, we looked at the procedures for considering a modification to the contract. Then, when appropriate, the process for modifying the contract.

Notes

Notes

Notes

Chapter 10 - Process and Procedures for Exercisi Option

Introduction

An option clause in the contract gives the Government the unilateral right, for a specified period of time, to:

- Elect to purchase additional supplies or services called for by the contract
- Extend the term of the contract

When it is determined by the Contracting Officer that exercising the option is in the best interest of the Government, a unilateral modification for the additional supplies, services, or contract term will be issued.

Process for Exercising an Option
1. Identify available options
2. Determine need for the supplies or services
3. Determine whether synopsis required
4. Determine the option price
5. Determine whether to exercise the option
6. Prepare a written determination
7. Prepare a notice to the contractor
8. Exercise the option

[handwritten margin note: Base period. (Base yr) + option yrs. sequentially added. (12 mo at a time)]

1. Identify available options

The standard FAR option clauses are:

- 52.217-6 Option for Increased Quantity
- 52.217-7 Option for Increased Quantity – Separately Priced Line Item
- 52.217-8 Option to Extend Services
- 52.217-9 Option to Extend the Term of the Contract

Example: You are administering a firm-fixed-price services contract which contains clause 52.217-8, Option to Extend Services. The contract expires 30 SEP 14. On your calendar, and in a memo to the contract file, you would identify 1 JUN 14 as your tracking date. This is approximately 120 days prior to the expiration of the contract term. On this date, you would begin discussions with the customer to identify if the services are still necessary. If the services are still necessary, and the contractor has been performing satisfactorily, you would then perform all the subsequent processes and procedures as discussed further in this chapter.

2. Determine need for the supplies or services

You must verify, by consulting the requiring activity, whether the need for additional supplies or services still exists. If yes, you also must establish that adequate funds are available by requesting a funding document from the customer. If no, then you will allow the contract to stand as is without ordering option quantities or extending the contract term.

3. Determine whether synopsis required

Normally, public notice to exercise an option is not required, as long as the original contract synopsis provided sufficient detail of the requirement, and was published in accordance with FAR Part 5.

4. Determine the option price

If the option(s) was not evaluated at the time of contract award, the Contracting Officer must determine if the option prices are fair and reasonable.

If option prices were considered and evaluated at the time of award, the option price could be a specific dollar amount or an amount to be determined by applying the provisions of a formula provided in the basic contract.

Even if the option prices were determined to be "fair and reasonable" at the time of contract award, those prices could be subject to adjustment under other clauses. For instance, the option prices could be subject to an Economic Price Adjustment provision or subject to change because of changes to prevailing labor rates provided by the Secretary of Labor on a service contract.

Example: You are administering a firm-fixed-price services contract that contains clause 52.217-8, Option to Extend Services. This clause states that the Government can order continued performance of the service at the specified contract rate. However, these rates may be adjusted because of revisions to the prevailing labor rates provided by the Secretary of Labor.

5. Determine whether to exercise the option

An informal analysis of prices in the current marketplace should be performed through market research to establish that the option price and offer is still the most advantageous to the Government.

The Government saves considerable time and administrative expense when exercising an option. If the market conditions have changed favorably for the supplies or services contained in the option, the savings realized by initiating a new procurement may be worth the time and expense associated with issuing a new solicitation, evaluating offers, and awarding a new contract.

6. Prepare a written determination

Once you have determined that it is in the best interest of the Government to exercise the option, the Contracting Officer shall make a written determination for the contract file (a memo to file) that exercise is in accordance with the:

- Terms of the option
- Requirements of FAR Part 17.206
    - o Funds are available
    - o The option fulfills an existing need
    - o The option is the most advantageous method of fulfilling the need
    - o The option was synopsized or exempted from synopsis in accordance with FAR Part 5
    - o Full and open competition requirements of FAR Part 6. Note: this requirement is determined to be fulfilled when the option was evaluated as part of the initial competition and you can determine the price fair and reasonable as discussed in the Determine the Option Price section above.

7. Prepare a notice to the contractor

Within the time specified in the option clause of the contract, the Contracting Officer shall provide written notice to the contractor when the determination has been made to exercise the option.

8. Exercise the option

If applicable, you may need to obtain a new wage determination from the Secretary of Labor, for option services that are subject to the Service Contract Act.

The SF 30 is normally used to execute the option modification. Option modifications, when issued within the time stated in the clause, are a unilateral modification.

Summary

You will exercise an option when the need still exists, the funds are available, and when it is in the best interest of the Government to do so.

The options are stated in the contract and are exercised only to the extent or within the parameters (time limits, price limits, quantity limits) established in the contract.

Notes

Notes

Notes

Chapter 11 - The Disputes Process

Disputes Resolution

The Government's policy is to try to resolve any and all contractual issues by mutual agreement at the Contracting Officer's level. This requires the use of fact-finding, research, and good negotiations strategies to resolve the disagreement. If the Contracting Officer fails to get a mutual agreement at that level, the contractor may seek resolution through the contract disputes process.

Definition of a Dispute

A dispute occurs when a controversy develops about the interpretation of payment, time, or money due to either party involved in a contract. A dispute, when unresolved, may lead to a claim. The claims process is authorized in the Contract Disputes Act (CDA) of 1978.

Contract Disputes Act (CDA)

Congress enacted the Contract Disputes Act in 1978. The act waives the Government's immunity and allows contractors to file claims or contest a Contracting Officer's actions as it relates to the contract. The CDA defines the responsibilities of the parties at each step of the disputes process, beginning with the initial action of the contractor in filing the claim with the Contracting Officer to the appeal process and associated legal forums.

The CDA provides jurisdiction to the Boards of Contract Appeals or the Court of Federal Claims (formally called the Court of Claims), When a contract dispute gets to the Court of Federal Claims, a judge acts as an independent third party who listens to both sides, reviews the issues and then renders a verdict.

What is a Claim?

A claim is a written demand or assertion by either the Government or the contractor seeking as a matter of right, the payment of money, the adjustment or interpretation of contract terms, or other relief arising under, or relating to the contract. FAR 33.201

A claim must be in writing and must contain sufficient detail to permit the Contracting Officer to give meaningful, reasonable consideration to the claim. The sufficiency of the case will be determined on a case by case basis.

FAR 33.201 further states, "a claim arising under a contract, (unlike a claim relating to that contract), is a claim that can be resolved under a contract clause that provides for the relief sought by the claimant (e.g., constructive changes, equitable adjustments, etc.). Claims "relating to" the contract, include but are not limited to, rescission, reformation, and breach of contract.

What is not a claim?

However, a written demand or written assertion by the contractor seeking the payment of money exceeding $100,000 must be certified under the Contract Disputes Act of 1978 and FAR 33.207. A voucher, invoice, or other routine request for payment that is not in dispute when submitted is not a claim. The submission may be converted to a claim, by written notice to the Contracting Officer as provided in FAR 33.206(a), if it is disputed either as to liability or amount or is not acted upon in a reasonable time.

What happens when a claim is filed?

When the Contracting Officer (CO) receives a claim, the determination whether the claim exceeds the dollar threshold for certification must be made. The CO ensures all supporting documentation is included with the written demand and that the demand meets the requirements of FAR 33.206 and 33.207. If the demand or supporting documentation is not in the correct format, it should be returned to the contractor for correction. This is important because the documents will become a part of the contract file and show evidence of the date of receipt of any submission from the contractor deemed to be a claim by the Contracting Officer. If the demand does not constitute a claim, then it is returned to the contractor, and the contractor is advised of the filing requirements.

Proper certification meeting the requirements of FAR 33.207 means:

1. A statement is provided that the claim is made in good faith
2. Supporting data are accurate and complete
3. The amount requested accurately reflects the contract adjustment for which the contractor believes the Government is liable
4. The signatory is duly authorized to certify the claim on behalf of the contractor

The Contracting Officer has no obligation to issue a final decision on any claim exceeding $100,000 that contains a defective certification, if, within 60 days after receipt of the claim, the Contracting Officer notifies the contractor, in writing, of the reasons why the claim was found to be defective.

If the contractor has certified a request for an equitable adjustment and desires to convert the request for equitable adjustment to a claim under the Contract Disputes Act, the contractor must certify the claim in accordance with FAR Subpart 33.2.

Resolve Disagreement before It Becomes a Claim

Make every reasonable effort to resolve disagreements or requests for equitable adjustment before they become claims. For example:

1. With other members of the Government acquisition team (e.g., the cognizant auditor), review the contractor's proposal/request
2. Collect other available information related to the proposal/request
3. Develop a Government position for negotiations or other method of resolution (e.g., mediation by a neutral party)
4. Resolve the disagreement.
5. Document the agreement in a bilateral contract modification,
6. Document the resolution process in the contract file using a price negotiation memorandum or similar document

Reject Any Claim That Is Not Timely

As stated in FAR 33.206, the Contracting Officer must issue a written decision on any Government claim initiated against a contractor within six years after accrual of the claim, unless the contracting parties agreed to a shorter time period. The six-year period does not apply to contracts awarded prior to October 1, 1995. The six-year statute of limitations does apply to fraud actions as well, except for Major fraud claims, (over $1M) and then the statute of limitation is seven years.

Contractor claims must be submitted, in writing, to the Contracting Officer for a decision within 6 years after accrual of a claim, unless the contracting parties agreed to a shorter time period. The contract file must be documented with evidence of the date of receipt of any submission from the contractor deemed to be a claim.

Prepare the Government's Position for the Dispute

The resolution of disagreements that lead to disputes under contracts may determine the amount or quality of work to be performed and the price to be paid. When interpreting contract clauses, there is no set of standard rules or well-defined analytical framework to follow as far as courts and boards of contract appeals are concerned.

Honest disputes over performance and the interpretation of contract clauses occur in the smoothest of contractual relationships. Even clear contract terms and conditions can give rise to the necessity of interpretation. A technique for avoiding a claim and settling a dispute may include continuing to consider, discuss, and negotiate the various elements of any disagreement, especially during the early stage of any potential controversy.

Claims Resolution

The Contracting Officer prepares the Government's position on the claim, after discussing it with the contractor. The discussion with the contractor affords the contractor the opportunity to provide all relevant facts on the situation. It also provides any additional information that the Contracting Officer may need before making the final decision. There may be the occasion when the claim is resolved informally. In the event the claim can be resolved, a modification or an implementation of an agreement on the claim will be incorporated into the contract.

Methods of Resolving Claims

There are four methods that can be used to resolve claims:

1. Informal discussion by direct negotiation between the parties
2. Alternative means of dispute resolution that involves an impartial third party who serves to assist the parties to resolve the issues in controversy, commonly known as Alternative Dispute Resolution (ADR)
3. Issuing a Contracting Officer's Final Decision (COFD)
4. Appellate process

Negotiation/Investigation

Negotiation is the preferred method to resolve a dispute before it results in a claim because the parties communicate and negotiate between themselves without any other party. Negotiation is also the least expensive method used to resolve a dispute. (In many cases, if a contractor submits a dispute, the Contracting Officer will be able to resolve the problem easily and at little cost in time and money if acted on it quickly. The Contracting Officer often can investigate the problem, determine where the fault lies, and get everything straight with a few telephone calls.) If the problem is more difficult than a simple misunderstanding, it may be possible to bring the parties together, discuss their points of view, and reach an acceptable compromise. Listening is a skill we can all improve upon. Many times if the contractor feels heard, regardless of our opinion, we will be able to reach an agreement/resolution. In fact, many contractor representatives need you to expressly tell them that you heard them, by saying, "What I hear you saying is: Is that right?" Then, if you have heard correctly, proceed with your position. Listening can be critical at this stage of the process. This may sound obvious, but it is amazing how failures to communicate speak/listen may cause issues that need never arise.

Alternative Disputes Resolution

The second method to resolve claims is through the use of Alternative Disputes Resolution (ADR). ADR defined in FAR 33.201, is any procedure voluntarily used to resolve issues in controversy without the need to resort to litigation. ADR procedures include assisted settlement negotiations, conciliation, facilitation, mediation, fact-finding, mini-trials, and arbitration.

As stated in FAR 33.214, the essential elements of ADR are:

1. The existence of an issue in controversy
2. A voluntary election by both parties to participate in the ADR process
3. An agreement on alternative procedures and terms to be used in the ADR process
4. Participation in the process by officials of both parties who have the authority to resolve the issue in controversy
5. Certification by the contractor in accordance with FAR 33.207, when using ADR procedures, to resolve all or part of a claim under the authority the Alternative Dispute Resolution (ADR) Act

FAR 33.214 states, requests for ADR are made by mutual consent of both parties. In any case, where a contractor rejects a request of an agency for ADR proceedings, the contractor shall inform the agency, in writing, of the contractor's specific reasons for rejecting the request. However, if the Contracting Officer rejects a small business contractor's request for ADR, the Contracting Officer must provide a written explanation to the other party, citing one of the following reasons for the rejections.

1. The need for an authoritative or definitive decision on a particular issue that has "precedential value," if the ADR proceeding is not likely to produce a result that is generally accepted as an authoritative precedent
2. When maintaining established policies is of special importance, "the need to minimize variations among individual decisions, if ADR proceedings are not likely to provide consistent results
3. The matter significantly affects others who are not parties to the ADR proceedings

Preparing The Contracting Officer's Final Decision

When a claim by or against a contractor cannot be settled by mutual agreement, and a decision on that claim is necessary, the Contracting Officer is required to issue a Contracting Officer Final Decision (COFD). A COFD may be a complete acceptance, partial acceptance, or a total rejection of the contractor's claim by the Government. Whether a claim belongs to the Government or to a contractor depends on who has the burden of proof concerning the particular issue. If the claim belongs to the contractor (i.e., Request for Equitable Adjustment (REA), T4C settlement proposals, etc.), then the disputes process cannot be initiated by the Government. Rather, the contractor must submit a claim to begin the disputes process. However, if the claim belongs to the Government (i.e., T4D, liquidated damages, breach of warranty, etc.), then a COFD is the first step in the litigation process.

In arriving at the final decision, the Contracting Officer shall review all the facts pertinent to the claim. The Government must ensure the appropriate FAR clauses are actually included in this particular contract, and actually have read the entire contract before issuing a COFD (particularly the Section H specialized clauses, that may contradict another section of the contract).

They should also obtain a legal review and a technical review as appropriate, and coordinate with the contract administration or contracting office, as well as any others with relevant information, as stated in FAR 33.211.

The final decision shall include:

1. A description of the claim
2. A reference to the pertinent contract terms
3. A statement of the factual areas of agreement and disagreement
4. A detailed statement of the Contracting Officer's final decision with supporting rationale
5. An advisement of the contractor's appeal rights

A demand for payment must be made when the COFD finds that the contractor is indebted to the Government. The interest on a Government's claim / COFD does not begin to run until the actual demand for payment is issued by the Government. This demand can be issued prior to the issuance of a COFD or can be included in the COFD. Failure to demand payment will result in the Government's loss of entitlement to any interest on its claim.

Failure to give a correct advisement of claimant's appellate rights may result in the final decision being considered inadequate to begin running of appellate time periods.

COFDs vary drastically in form and content. Some are lengthy and detailed; others short and abrupt. Much depends on the complexity of the issues presented and the inclinations of the individual Contracting Officer. Regardless of its length or detail, the decision should be unbiased and impartial and the independent judgment of the Contracting Officer. It should be written in a logical and understandable manner and must address each and every aspect of the contractor's claim. The analysis process leading up to a COFD is categorized and can be found in FAR 33.211.

The Contracting Officer must issue the final decision as follows:

- For claims equal to or less than $100,000, a COFD must be issued within 60 days after receiving a written request/claim from the contractor.
- For claims greater than $100,000, a decision should be issued within 60 days after receipt of a certified claim. However, if the final decision cannot be rendered within 60 days, the Contracting Officer must notify the contractor within 60 days as to a specific date in the future when the final decision will be issued. We should only take a reasonable period of time to issue our final decision.

Contracting Officer's Final Decision and How to Initiate Payment of Any Amount

As stated in FAR 33.211, the Contracting Officer will issue a final decision within a reasonable time, taking into account the size and complexity of the claim, the adequacy of the contractor's supporting data and any other relevant factors. If the Contracting Officer delays issuing a final decision on a claim, the contractor may request that the agency board or court direct the Contracting Officer to issue a final decision within a specified time period. Any failure of the Contracting Officer to issue a final decision within the required time periods will be deemed a decision by the Contracting Officer denying the claim (deemed denial) and will authorize the contractor to file an appeal or suit on the claim.

The COFD should be sent to the contractor by certified mail with a return receipt requested. The receipt provides proof of when the contractor's appeal rights period begins, and proof that the Contracting Officer was within the statutory limitations for issuing a final decision.

As stated in FAR 33.208, the Government shall pay interest on a contractor's claim on the amount found due and unpaid from the date that the Contracting Officer receives the claim, or payment is otherwise due, if that date is later until the date of payment. Simple interest on claims shall be paid at the rate fixed by the Secretary of the Treasury as provided in the Contract Disputes Act.

The Appeal Process

A Contracting Officer's final decision is final and conclusive. It is not subject to review by any forum, tribunal, or Government agency unless appealed by the contractor after receipt of the decision to either a board of contract appeals within 90 days or the United States Court of Federal Claims within 12 months. An appeal made to a board of contract appeals is considered an administrative review while an appeal to the United States Court of Federal Claims is a judicial review. The contractor's election of the forum is binding. Once the choice of forum is made, the contractor is excluded from pursuing the claim in the other court, regardless whether there is still time available to do so. Hence, if the ASBCA dismissed a contractor's claim and there was still time left to file with the Federal Court (12 months), too bad! The contractor cannot do so!

Decisions of the Court of Appeals for the Federal Circuit (CAFC) may not be automatically appealed to the Supreme Court. The Supreme Court elects which appeals it wants to hear.

The duties of the Contracting Officer upon the appeal are outlined in FAR 33.212, which requires the Contracting Officer to prepare the claims file. This is sometimes referred to as the Rule 4 file, which should be reviewed by the contracting legal office for acceptability. FAR 33.213 requires the Contracting Officer to continue to finance the ongoing performance of the contract. The contractor is required to continue performance and to comply with any decision of the Contracting Officer pending a final decision on an appeal under the contract.

For further information:

Court of Federal Claims
http://www.uscfc.uscourts.gov

Court of Appeals for the Federal Circuit
http://www.fedcir.gov/http://www.cafc.uscourts.gov

Notes

Notes

Notes

Notes

Chapter 12 - Alternative Dispute Resolution (ADR

ADR Background

One consequence of the dispute process is that it can require an excessive amount of time, money, and resources. In the U.S. Court of Federal Claims, some disputes have taken as long as 25 years to resolve. The Armed Services Board of Contract Appeals was established as an informal, speedy alternative, but has evolved into a complex court-like system that can be both expensive and time-consuming to use. Many contractors can no longer afford the financial burden and other resources necessary to receive a fair hearing in one of these forums. Even for the government, the delays in obtaining decisions, the cost of the litigation, and the disruption to program and procurement personnel in supporting the litigation have often become prohibitive. When the Government and a contractor cannot reach agreement on some issue under a contract, and it turns into a formal dispute, some things to consider are what impact the dispute will have on the day to day working relationship between the two parties. Also, the sheer cost in terms of time, money, and other resources that have to be redirected into the dispute process should motivate both parties to reach agreement.

When litigation is used, the only certain result is a destroyed relationship between the contractor and the Government. Litigation is combat; one party will win, and the other will lose. Once the process starts, it rarely brings about a cooperative and mutually satisfactory resolution. Even when a settlement is reached, it is often on the courthouse steps just before trial and after costly and time-consuming pre-trial preparation had been completed.

Congress recognized that ADR procedures result in decisions that are faster, less expensive, and less contentious than the traditional agency dispute resolution proceedings. The Administrative Disputes Resolution Act (ADRA) of 1996 required agencies to develop policies and training and to take measures to promote the use of ADR. This legislation promoted a national policy to promote ADR that is supported by a number of other laws, Executive Orders, regulations, and policies.

What is ADR?

ADR is defined as any procedure that is used in lieu of litigation to resolve issues in controversy. These methods include, but are not limited to, fact-finding, facilitation mediation, arbitration, mini-trials, settlement negotiations, conciliation, early neutral evaluations, or any combination of these methods. These various procedures fall into three general categories.

1. Cooperative decision making where parties resolve disputes unassisted
2. Third-party assistance with relationship building, procedural, or substantive issues
3. Third-party for making a decision on the merits of a case

Fact-finding

Fact-finding is a process in which a neutral party collects information about a dispute and provides a report to the disputing parties. At the option of the parties, the report may include recommendations regarding how the dispute might be resolved. As mentioned above, this might be the first opportunity to hear the contractor's position truly. Listening skills can prove quite beneficial here.

Facilitation

Facilitation is the use of a third party to assist the parties to enhance information exchange or promote effective decision making. The party is impartial and lacks decision-making authority toward the issues and topics under discussion. The facilitator's expertise provides information exchange, uses problem-solving skills, and improves decision making processes of the parties. The goal is to help the parties define clear statements of desired outcomes.

Mediation

One familiar method of third party assisted procedures is mediation. In mediation, a neutral party assists disputants in articulating and understanding each other's positions with the ultimate goal of reaching solutions that will preserve the parties' key interests. The process is voluntary and usually conducted in confidence with the parties maintaining complete control over the outcome. The neutral mediator serves at the convenience of the disputants who can make the selection of one on whatever criteria they find important. Once selected, the mediator helps organize the negotiation into a structured process that minimizes hostility and maximizes the exchange of relevant information. The emphasis is on options and remedies for the future that will satisfy both parties. Again listening skills are critical here.

Arbitration

Another well-known method of ADR that also involves a third party, quite different from mediation, is arbitration. Instead of merely helping the parties negotiate and find common ground for a settlement, an arbitrator or panel of arbitrators is usually given decision-making power by the parties. The arbitrator may be authorized in advance by the parties to make specific findings, or simply to decide which party is correct. The arbitrator may be given the power (or the duty) to require each party to submit one "best and final" proposed resolution of the dispute, with the arbitrator, then selecting the proposal that it considers to be the fairest. An arbitration decision can be either binding or nonbinding.

Mini-Trial

The mini-trial is a hybrid dispute resolution process that it involves a data presentation component similar to litigation, a negotiation component, and the potential for third-party mediation and advisory opinion. It is the process where the dispute is presented to a third party neutral by representatives from both parties assisted by a neutral advisor.

A mini-trial is not a trial since it does not use a judge or lengthy procedures. Instead, it is a short hearing, usually lasting about a day, in which a lawyer or spokesperson for each party presents evidence in support of its position concerning certain specified issues. A "neutral advisor" agreed upon by the parties may be used to assist representatives of each party in understanding not only the issues but also the strengths and weaknesses of the party's positions as reflected in the evidence.

Summary

In this chapter, we first looked at the fundamental causes of disputes and claims between the contractor and the Government. We discussed how the Contract Disputes Act and the Disputes clause govern the actions of both the Government and the contractor. You learned that:

- The Government's policy is to try to resolve all contractual issues by mutual agreement at the Contracting Officer's level.
- A dispute is formed under a contract when a controversy develops as to the interpretation of payment, time, or money due to either party. A dispute, when unresolved, may lead to a claim.
- A claim is a written demand or assertion by either the Government or the contractor seeking as a matter of right, the payment of money, the adjustment or interpretation of contract terms, or other relief arising under, or relating to the contract.
- A written demand or written assertion by the contractor seeking the payment of money exceeding $100,000 is not a claim under the Contract Disputes Act of 1978 until certified as required by the Act and FAR 33.207.
- When the Contracting Officer (CO) receives a claim, the determination whether the claim exceeds the dollar threshold for certification must be made. The CO ensures all supporting documentation is included with the written demand and that the demand meets the requirements of FAR 33.206 and 33.207.
- You need to make every reasonable effort to resolve disagreements or requests for equitable adjustment before they become claims.
- As stated in FAR 33.206, the Contracting Officer must issue a written decision on any Government claim initiated against a contractor within six years after accrual of the claim, unless the contracting parties agreed to a shorter time period. The six-year period does not apply to contracts awarded prior to October 1, 1995.

We discussed the methods that may be employed to resolve claims. When it comes to resolving claims, you learned that there are four methods that can be used to resolve claims:

1. An informal discussion by direct negotiation between the parties

2. Alternative means of dispute resolution that involves an impartial third party who serves to assist the parties to resolve the issues in controversy, commonly known as Alternative Dispute Resolution (ADR)

3. Issuing a Contracting Officer's Final Decision (COFD)

4. Appellate process

You discovered that:

*   Negotiation is the preferred method to resolve a dispute before it results in a claim because the parties communicate and negotiate between themselves without any other party.
*   The second method to resolve claims is through the use of Alternative Disputes Resolution (ADR). ADR defined in FAR 33,201, is any procedure voluntarily used to resolve issues in controversy without the need to resort to litigation. ADR procedures include assisted settlement negotiations, conciliation, facilitation, mediation, fact-finding, mini-trials, and arbitration.
*   When a claim by or against a contractor cannot be settled by mutual agreement, and a decision on that claim is necessary, the Contracting Officer is required to issue a Contracting Officer Final Decision (COFD). A COFD may be a complete acceptance, partial acceptance, or a total rejection of the contractor's claim by the Government.
*   A Contracting Officer's final decision is final and conclusive. It is not subject to review by any forum, tribunal, or Government agency unless appealed by the contractor after receipt of the decision to either a board of contract appeals within 90 days or the United States Court of Federal Claims within 12 months.
*   An appeal made to a board of contract appeals is considered an administrative review while an appeal to the United States Court of Federal Claims is a judicial review. The contractor's election of the forum is binding. Once the choice of forum is made, the contractor is excluded from pursuing the claim in the other court, whether or not there is still time available to do so.
*   We learned that, of the methods discussed, direct negotiation and ADR are the preferred methods of claim resolution.

Finally, we covered the different methods of ADR. You learned that:

- ADR is defined as any procedure that is used in lieu of litigation to resolve issues in controversy. These methods include, but are not limited to, fact-finding, facilitation mediation, arbitration, mini-trials, settlement negotiations, conciliation, early neutral evaluations, or any combination of these methods.
- Fact-finding is a process in which a neutral party collects information about a dispute and provides a report to the disputing parties.
- Facilitation is the use of a third party to assist the parties to enhance information exchange or promote effective decision making.
- One familiar method of third party assisted procedures is mediation. In mediation, a neutral party assists disputants in articulating and understanding each other's' positions with the ultimate goal of reaching solutions that will preserve the parties' key interests. The process is voluntary and usually conducted in confidence with the parties maintaining complete control over the outcome.
- Another well-known method of ADR that involves a third party, quite different from mediation, is arbitration. Instead of merely helping the parties negotiate and find common ground for a settlement, an arbitrator or panel of arbitrators is usually given decision-making power by the parties.

The mini-trial is a hybrid dispute resolution process that it involves a data presentation component similar to litigation, a negotiation component, and the potential for third-party mediation and an advisory opinion. It is the process where the dispute is presented to a third party neutral by representatives from both parties assisted by a neutral advisor.

Notes

Notes

Notes

Chapter 13 - Contract Closeout

Introduction

Closeout is the Government's process to confirm that there are no uncompleted contractual obligations of either the Government or the contractor. Closeout ensures that the correct final payment is made to the vendor and the correct deliverables are received by the Government. All contractual obligations at contract closeout must be discharged through final payment, release, or accord and satisfaction.

Importance of Contract Closeout

FAR 4.804 sets specific time periods for closing contracts. Timely closeout deobligates excess funds and returns remaining funds for possible use elsewhere. It also minimizes the costs associated with administration and closeout processes. This benefits all parties and allows all affected activities to concentrate on current and future requirements. The time period for closing a contract is based on both the type of contract and date of physical completion. A contract is considered to be physically complete when:

- The contractor has completed the required deliveries, and the Government has inspected and accepted the supplies.
- The contractor has performed all services, and the Government has accepted these services.
- All Option provisions, if any, have expired.
- The Government has given the contractor a notice of complete contract termination.

Facilities contracts and rentals, use, and storage agreements are considered to be physically complete when:

- The Government has given the contractor a notice of complete contract termination.
- The contract period has expired.

FAR 4.804-5 Procedures for Closing out Contract Files

(a) The contract administration office is responsible for initiating (automated or manual) administrative closeout of the contract after receiving evidence of its physical completion. At the outset of this process, the contract administration office must review the contract funds status and notify the contracting office of any excess funds the contract administration office might deobligate.

When complete, the administrative closeout procedures must ensure that—

(1) Disposition of classified material is completed;

(2) *Final patent report is cleared.* If a final patent report is required, the contracting officer may proceed with contract closeout in accordance with the following procedures, or as otherwise prescribed by agency procedures:

(i) Final patent reports should be cleared within 60 days of receipt.

(ii) If the final patent report is not received, the contracting officer shall notify the contractor of the contractor's obligations and the Government's rights under the applicable patent rights clause, in accordance with 27.303. If the contractor fails to respond to this notification, the contracting officer may proceed with contract closeout upon consultation with the agency legal counsel responsible for patent matters regarding the contractor's failure to respond.

(3) Final royalty report is cleared;

(4) There is no outstanding value engineering change proposal;

(5) Plant clearance report is received;

(6) Property clearance is received;

(7) All interim or disallowed costs are settled;

(8) Price revision is completed;

(9) Subcontracts are settled by the prime contractor;

(10) Prior year indirect cost rates are settled;

(11) Termination docket is completed;

(12) Contract audit is completed;

(13) Contractor's closing statement is completed;

 (14) Contractor's final invoice has been submitted; and

(15) Contract funds review is completed and excess funds deobligated.

(b) When the actions in paragraph (a) of this subsection have been verified, the contracting officer administering the contract must ensure that a contract completion statement, containing the following information, is prepared:

(1) Contract administration office name and address (if different from the contracting office).

(2) Contracting office name and address.

(3) Contract number.

(4) Last modification number.

(5) Last call or order number.

(6) Contractor name and address.

(7) The dollar amount of excess funds, if any.

(8) Voucher number and date, if final payment has been made.

(9) Invoice number and date, if the final approved invoice has been forwarded to a disbursing office of another agency or activity and the status of the payment is unknown.

(10) A statement that all required contract administration actions have been fully and satisfactorily accomplished.

(11) Name and signature of the contracting officer.

(12) Date.

(c) When the statement is completed, the contracting officer must ensure that—

(1) The signed original is placed in the contracting office contract file (or forwarded to the contracting office for placement in the files if the contract administration office is different from the contracting office); and

(2) A signed copy is placed in the appropriate contract administration file if administration is performed by a contract administration office.

Time Standards for Closing Contracts

In accordance with FAR 4.804, there are different time standards for closing contracts based upon the type of contract file. The following table illustrates the different standards:

(A) Type of Contract File	(B) Closed When Contracting Officer:	(C) Timeframe to Close Contract
Simplified Acquisition Procedures (SAP)	Receives evidence of receipt of property and final payment	When (B) is satisfied
Firm-Fixed Price (other than SAP)	Receives evidence of receipt of physical completion	Month when (B) is satisfied plus 6 months
Contracts requiring settlement of direct cost rates	Receives evidence of receipt of physical completion	Month when (B) is satisfied plus 36 months
All other contract types	Receives evidence of receipt of physical completion	Month when (B) is satisfied plus 20 months

Fixed Price Closeout

Difficulties encountered in closing out fixed-price contracts are likely associated with documentation of deliverables with unliquidated obligation balances (excess funds).

Contract Funds Status Review

FAR 4.804-5 explains that once a CMO receives evidence of physical completion, you shall review the contract funds status and notify the PCO of any excess funds available for deobligation at the outset of the closeout process. When excess or negative unliquidated funds exist, a funds review should be performed at the Accounting Classification Reference Number (ACRN) level to determine the cause, i.e.:

- If it is determined those excess funds are a result of unperformed work due to a specific line item or deliverable on the contract, these should be removed and the ACO shall issue a modification accomplishing the deobligation. The CMO is no longer required to obtain PCO authorization prior to deobligating excess funds.

Administrative Closeout Procedures

Among the administrative closeout procedures, Government Furnished Property (GFP), Classified Material, and Final Patents/Royalty Reports will be discussed.

Government Property

In accordance with FAR 4.804-5, administrative contract procedures must ensure that all Government Furnished Property (GFP) has been dispositioned.

Final Patent/Royalty Reports

All Final Patent/Royalty Reports have been obtained and forwarded to the buying activity. If the contract contains FAR 52.227-11, Patent Rights Retention by the Contractor, a final patent report is required only if there is an invention.

Cost-Reimbursable Closeouts

Cost-type contracts are usually the most complex contracts to administer and to close. They rely upon actual costs, which may not be agreed to, for years after physical completion. There are several initiatives in place that would preclude delays in settling indirect cost rates. However, to prevent closeout problems, the contractor and contract should be monitored.

Monitoring Cost-Reimbursable Contracts

Contractor areas that should be monitored include:

- Indirect Cost Settlement
    - What year are rates settled through?
    - Are there any overdue cost proposals?
    - What is the status of final voucher submission, by fiscal year?
- Corporate Allocations
- Utilization of Quick Closeout

Monitoring Individual Contracts

It is helpful when individual contracts are monitored in the following areas:

- Period of Performance
- Timely Submittal of Required Reports and Data Items
- Funding Status
    - Total Obligations by ACRN
    - Canceling Funds Identified
    - Current Funding Balance Correct in MOCAS
- Public Vouchers
- Previous Amounts Paid
- Obligated Funds Correct
- Fee Withholding, if any, Identified and Correct

By monitoring contractor and individual contract status, the problems associated with the closeout process, including final reconciliation of funds, will be minimal.

As stated in the section on Firm-Fixed Price closeout procedures, the same issues of Government-furnished property, classified material, and final patent/royalty reports need to be resolved in cost reimbursable closeouts.

Submission of Final Voucher

The closeout procedures also include ensuring that:

Contractor's final invoice has been submitted. Once indirect cost rates are settled for all contractor years with contract performance, a contractor has 120 days to submit a final voucher and closing package to the ACO for audit review and ACO approval for payment. (The "contractor years" is a period determined by each contractor, i.e., Jan-Dec or Mar-Feb versus the Government's fiscal year, Oct-Sep.)

Final Voucher –Review/Approval

ACO review/approval of a final voucher is required as a step of closeout procedures. The steps include:

- Verification that all contractual requirements have been satisfied
- Completion of any fee adjustments
- Verification that contractual funding limitations have not been exceeded
- Identification of the application of any DFAS offsets
- Verification of accuracy of Contractor Release and Assignment
- Verification that all previous contractor vouchers have been paid
- Verification that the final voucher is identified as a "Final Voucher" and has a "Z" next to the voucher number
- Approval for payment with ACO signature and date
- Deobligation modification processed and distributed for any funds determined to be excess
- Forward the final voucher to the payment office for processing

For Level of Effort (LOE), this clause requires fee adjustments based on the number of hours actually expended. The clause may apply to individual task orders, or it may apply to the contract as a whole. (See FAR 16.207 for LOE but refer to contract for specific clause). Level of Effort can be defined as follows: the contractor is to provide a specified level of effort, over a stated period of time, on work that can be stated only in general terms; and the Government is to pay the contractor a fixed dollar amount.

Canceled Funds (Replacement Funds Required)

If adequate funding was on the contract but has since been canceled, the ACO will submit the final voucher to DFAS for payment. The voucher will reject for insufficient funds.

Time and Material/Labor-Hour Closeout

Time and Material (T&M) and Labor Hour (LH) contracts offer unique challenges for closeout. A T&M contract provides no positive profit incentive to the contractor for cost control or labor efficiency. The labor-hours contract is a variation of the T&M contract differing only in that materials are not supplied by the contractor.

The ACO should monitor not-to-exceed amounts on labor and other direct costs (i.e., material and travel), to ensure contractor billing is in accordance with the contract.

Fixed Indirect Rates

When the indirect rates are fixed in the contract, the contractor should prepare a final voucher for each contract or task order upon physical completion. The ACO should then ascertain whether a discrepancy exists and an audit is necessary.

It is suggested that the following areas be considered when reviewing the final voucher:

- Total Labor Hours Required by Contract
- Total Labor Hours Expended
- Total Cost of Material
- Level of Effort

For example, the ACO reviews the total hours expended with what is required by the contract. If they don't match, the contractor may be expending more hours than allowed by the contract. If the contractor's accounting and labor recording systems are inadequate (i.e., if the direct costs are not properly segregated from indirect cost; a timekeeping system does not identify employee's labor by intermediate or final cost objectives, etc.), the ACO should consider the nature of the inadequacy prior to determining whether to forward for audit.

Quick Closeout

The quick closeout process offers an alternative to holding contracts open until indirect cost rates are settled. When it becomes apparent that there will be a delay in settlement of final indirect rates, it is recommended that the ACO utilize quick closeout where applicable.

FAR Quick Closeout Regulations

The Quick Closeout procedures are identified in FAR 42.708. Specifically, quick closeout procedures may be used if:

- The contract is physically complete.
- The amount of unsettled indirect cost to be allocated to the contract is relatively insignificant. Indirect cost amounts are insignificant when:
- The total unsettled indirect cost to be allocated to anyone contract does not exceed $1 million.
- Unless otherwise provided in agency procedures, the cumulative unsettled indirect cost to be allocated to one or more contracts in a single fiscal year does not exceed 15% of the estimated total unsettled indirect costs allocable to cost-type contracts for that fiscal year. The Contracting Officer may waive the 15% restriction based upon risk assessment that considers contractor's accounting, estimating, and purchasing systems; other concerns of the cognizant contract auditors, and any other pertinent information.
- Agreement can be reached on a reasonable estimate of allocable dollars.

Quick Closeout not a Binding Precedent

Unlike early closeout procedures, the determinations of final indirect costs under quick closeout procedures are final for the contracts this procedure covers, and no adjustments are made to other contracts for over or under-recoveries of costs allocated or allocable to the contracts covered by the advance agreement. Indirect cost rates used in the quick closeout of a contract are not considered a binding precedent when establishing the final indirect cost rates for other contracts.

Identifying Quick Closeout Candidates

The quick closeout candidates can be identified in various ways by the PCO, ACO, or the contractor:

- **PCO**. A PCO will sometimes contact an ACO concerning closeout status of a particular contract and will often inquire about quick closeout possibilities.
- **ACO**. The ACO usually is the primary person who can identify candidates for quick closeout. The ACO should consider the volume of contracts awaiting settlement of indirect rates and affected by canceling funds. Quick closeout is an excellent way to close contracts and preclude millions of dollars from canceling. Another area that ACOs may consider is time and material type contracts. These contracts are ideal for quick closeout because the only redeterminable amount is usually the general and administrative (G&A) costs associated with the other direct costs (ODCs) in the contract.
- **Contractor**. The contractor occasionally will request quick closeout procedures for a given contract or group of contracts.

Negotiating Quick Closeout Rates

Once the quick closeout candidates are identified, the ACO should coordinate with the contractor before beginning the negotiation of quick closeout rates.

1. The first step the ACO should take is to contact the contractor regarding quick-closeout procedures officially. The letter should include the list of contracts and should request the following information:

    *   Proposed/Certified indirect cost rates for three years preceding the fiscal year for which you are pursuing quick closeout.
    *   The settled indirect cost rates for three years preceding the fiscal year for which you are pursuing quick closeout
    *   The calculated variance factor between the proposed and settled rates
    *   The proposed/certified indirect cost rates covering the period of performance for the referenced contracts
    *   Contract status of each contract.

2. Second, once the ACO receives the indirect cost history for the last three settled years, an analysis should be performed. It is important to analyze the contractor's history of proposing rates higher than the final determined rates in the past three years; the ACO can use a decrement factor. The decrement factor is the difference between the proposed/certified rates and the settled rates; it is used on their unsettled year by either establishing a decrement factor or applying a percentage of the difference. By using a decrement, the ACO will ensure that the Government's financial interest is protected. The decrement factor is the most commonly used means of establishing a fair and equitable quick closeout rate. Some alternative rate sources are:

    *   The final indirect cost rates agreed upon for the immediately preceding fiscal year
    *   The provisional billing rates for the current fiscal year
    *   Estimated rates for the final fiscal year of contract performance based on the contractor's actual data adjusted for any historical disallowance found in prior years.

3. The final step is the negotiation of a quick closeout rate. The actual negotiation can be conducted by telephone.

Preparing an Advance Agreement

Once an agreement is reached for the final rate, the ACO should prepare an advance agreement. Both the contractor and the ACO should sign the agreement.

Situations When Contract Closeouts are Delayed

Traditional closeout procedures are, for the most part, dictated by the payment clauses contained in affected contracts. When the circumstances mentioned below exist, it is sometimes virtually impossible to close contracts using traditional methods. In these instances, the ACO shall perform a cost risk analysis and exercise business judgment in accordance with FAR 1.602-2 to ensure that the Government's interests are protected, and administrative actions are reasonable. With the goal of minimizing loss to the Government, exercising and implementing efficient business practices and processes, the following guidelines are offered as a solution to these "problem closures."

Solutions for Problem Closures

A "problem closure" is considered to be a contract that has unusual circumstances barring the use of traditional closeout methods.

Unusual Circumstance	Possible Solution
1. Contractor is No Longer in Business	Administrative Unilateral Closeout
2. Contractor is Bankrupt	Coordinate with Office of General Counsel
3. Contractor Has Failed to Submit Indirect Cost Data	Notify Contractor of Internal Control Deficiency; Decrement Current Billing Rates; Unilateral Determination of Indirect Cost Rates; Unilateral Determination of Final Rates/Prices
4. Contractor is Unable to Submit Supporting Indirect Cost Data	Administrative Unilateral Closeout
5. Contractor Has Failed to Submit Final Invoice/Voucher	Fixed Price Contracts – Administrative Unilateral Closeout Cost Reimbursable Contracts – Accelerated Final Voucher Preparation/Review

Summary

Traditional closeout procedures are, for the most part, dictated by the payment clauses contained in affected contracts. We looked at some of the situations when a contract closeout is delayed. Eventually, when the unusual circumstances have been resolved, the contract will then be able to be closed out.

Notes

Notes

Notes

Notes

Chapter 14 - Terminations

Termination for Default

Termination for default is based on the contractual right of the Government to terminate, in whole or in part, the contractor's right to proceed in instances where the contractor fails to perform its contractual obligations.

If, after termination for default, it is determined that the contractor was not in default or that the default was excusable, the termination for default will be considered a termination for convenience and the rights of the parties will be governed by the termination for convenience clause.

If the contract does not include a termination for convenience clause, the contract will be equitably adjusted to compensate for the "improper" termination for default.

The default clauses applicable to fixed-price service, supply, construction, and R&D contracts all provide for such compensation. The termination clause for cost-reimbursement contracts is unique in that it includes both default and convenience features. These clauses create an administrative means to terminate a contract and settle fairly, thus avoiding lawsuits by or against the Government.

The contract may be revived by mutual agreement in certain cases where the Contracting Officer determines it to be in the Government's best interest.

The general principles of contract termination hold that the Government's has a right to terminate for default is based on the contractor's failure to:

- Perform on time, as provided in the contract
- Perform any other provision of the contract
- Make progress, to the extent that the delay endangers contract performance.

Although not expressly provided for in the default clause, the Government may immediately terminate for default if the contractor definitely exhibits an intention not to perform within the time fixed in the contract. This manifested intention is termed as anticipatory breach or repudiation. It should also be noted that the Contracting Officer may terminate a contract for default if the contractor submits a false claim, or has committed fraud against the Government, or is found to be involved in a conflict of interest.

Terminations:
1. for default
2. for cause. (commercial)
3. for convenience.

A termination for default has these consequences:

- The contractor must return un-liquidated progress or advance payments
- The Government does not have to pay the costs of uncompleted work, but only the costs of products delivered to and accepted by the Government. In the case of a cost-reimbursement contract, the Government is liable for costs incurred up to the date of termination, plus a proportional part of any fee. The Government is not liable for settlement expenses, or for any profit on costs of preparation for work in progress.
- The Government has the right to take over the contractor's inventory, subject to a negotiated compensation
- The contractor is liable for any excess costs the Government may have to pay for reacquiring supplies or services. (Under a cost-reimbursement contract, the Government has no right to reacquire; therefore, the contractor has no liability for excess costs.)
- The contractor may also be liable for breach of contract damages.

Alternatives to Termination for Default

Default is rarely the best solution for resolving unsatisfactory contractor performance. Rather, default termination is considered to be the only way to get the work done after considering all other alternatives. Even where the Government is successful in defaulting, reacquiring, and collecting excess costs, it will not receive the supplies or services under contract when it wants them. Further, the Government may suffer a serious loss of time and may be put to considerable effort and expense in defending its default and repurchase actions.

Procedures for Termination for Default

The Government must follow the procedural requirements of the default clause to effect a proper termination.

Preliminary Notice

If the basis for default is failure to deliver or to perform on time, the Government is not required to give any notice of failure or of the possibility of default prior to issuing the termination for default notice itself. However, if the Government fails to enforce the provisions relating to timely delivery or takes any other action that might be construed as a waiver of the delivery or performance date, it must then send a preliminary notice to the contractor, proposing or setting a new date. This notice should call the contractor's attention to his or her liabilities in the event of default termination and request an explanation of the failure. The notice may invite the contractor in for a conference.

Cure Notice

In a case where the contractor fails to perform some provision other than those dealing with timely delivery, or so fails to make progress as to endanger performance altogether, the Government must give the contractor notice of the failure and allow at least 10 days for cure (remedy of the failure before issuing a termination notice. This "10-day cure notice" should:

- State that a termination for default may arise unless the failure to perform or make adequate progress is cured within 10 days (or such longer period as the Contracting Officer may grant)
- Call the contractor's attention to his or her contractual liabilities in the event of default
- Request an explanation of the failure to perform
- State that failure to present an explanation may be taken as an admission that there is no valid explanation
- Where appropriate, invite the contractor to discuss the matter at a conference

Show Cause Notice

If the time remaining in the contract delivery schedule is not sufficient to permit a realistic "cure" period of 10 days or more, a "Show Cause Notice" may be used. It should be sent immediately upon expiration of the delivery period.

Notice of Termination for Default

Once the Contracting Officer determines that termination for default would be proper, he or she must issue an official notice of termination that:

- Sets forth the contract number and data and describes the acts or omissions that constitute the default
- States that the contractor's right to proceed with performance of the contract (or a portion of the contract) is terminated
- States that if the Contracting Officer has not determined whether the failure to perform is excusable, it is possible that the contractor will be held liable for any excess costs the Government must pay in reacquiring terminated supplies or services
- States that if the Contracting Officer determines that failure to perform is inexcusable:
    1. Notice of termination constitutes such a determination and is a final decision under the disputes clause
    2. The contractor will be held liable for any excess costs of reacquisition
    3. The contractor has the right to appeal under the disputes clause
- States the Government reserves all rights and remedies provided by law or under contract
- States that the notice represents a decision that the contractor is in default as specified and that it has the right to appeal under the disputes clause

Excusable Defaults

Under the default clause, the contractor has certain defenses in response to the Government's notice of termination for default. It only takes one viable defense to overturn the default termination and convert it to one for the convenience of the Government.

The contractor cannot be terminated for default if the failure to perform arises out of causes beyond its control and without its fault or negligence. If failure to perform is caused by the default of a subcontractor (at any tier), and if it arises out of causes beyond the control of both the contractor and subcontractor and without the fault or negligence of either of them, then the contractor still cannot be terminated for default.

This does not hold true if the supplies or services to be furnished by the subcontractor were obtainable from other sources in time to permit the contractor to meet the required delivery schedule.

Essentially the same provision is found in the excusable delays clause applicable to cost-reimbursement contracts. To simplify:

- A contractor's default is excusable if it is not caused by either contracting party or if it is caused by the Government
- A contractor's default is inexcusable if caused by the contractor's own fault or negligence, by something or somebody within its control, or by one of its subcontractors

The excusable delay section of the default clause lists several excusable causes, some of which are:

- Acts of God or the public enemy
- Acts of the Government in either its sovereign or contractual capacity
- Fires, floods, epidemics, and quarantine restrictions
- Strikes, freight embargoes, and unusually severe weather

In each such case, however, the failure to perform must be beyond the control and without the fault or negligence of the contractor. Furthermore, the excusable cause must be the proximate (direct) cause of the failure to perform.

If actions of both parties contribute to the default and individual causes and effects of the responsibilities of each party are "so intertwined as to defy disentanglement," then the contractor's default will not be excusable.

Termination despite an Excusable Delay

If the Contracting Officer determines, before issuance of a notice of termination, that the contractor's failure is excusable, but that termination is still in the best interest of the Government, he or she can take one of two actions:

1. Terminate for convenience
2. Terminate at no cost to either party

Prior to issuance of the termination notice, when the Contracting Officer has not been able to determine whether the contractor's default is excusable, he or she will make a written decision as soon as possible. The decision will promptly be given to the contractor, who will be advised of its right to appeal under the disputes clause.

Waiver of Default

After the contractor is in default, the Government's rights may be waived:

1. If the Government does something or fails to do something that encourages the contractor to continue performance
2. If the contractor, relying on that encouragement, continues to exert effort and incur costs in the performance of the contract

If, after default, a contractor continues to spend money and to perform, the Board of Contract Appeals will scrutinize anything the Contracting Officer said or did, and failed to say or do, that may have induced or encouraged the contractor to continue. If the Board finds evidence of such encouragement, a waiver may result.

If, after default, the contractor does no more work and incurs no further expenses, then, regardless of what the Contracting Officer does (sending letters urging the contractor to continue, or in any other way encouraging continued performance), there will normally be no waiver. The Government's right to terminate for default will remain intact.

The following actions on the part of Government personnel have been held to waive a default:

- Accepting late delivery
- Ordering and accepting corrective actions after default
- Encouraging continued performance, providing the contractor does then continue
- Negotiating a revised delivery schedule
- Revising other contract terms
- Failure of the Government to timely assert or otherwise protect its contractual rights

The following kinds of conduct on the part of Government personnel have been held not to waive a default:

- Merely inquiring as to when delivery/performance could be made
- Attempting unsuccessfully to revise other contract terms

The best way to avoid waiver of default is to have good rapport and communication between the contracting office and the program office. This aids all personnel who are involved with the contractor to know contract status, the Government's position, and what each party is supposed to do and not do. Above all else, the Contracting Officer, as the agent of the Government authorized to issue a default termination, must be kept fully informed of any performance problem.

When it is concluded that the Government's action or failure to act is grounds for a waiver of the contractor's default, the Contracting Officer should take immediate steps to establish a new delivery schedule. These steps will revive the Government's right to terminate for default so that right is available in the event of a new default.

Termination for Convenience

Under the termination for convenience clause, the Government has a right to cancel work under a contract whenever it determines that it is in its best interest. Such a decision is a unilateral right of the Government.

It is not a decision to be made lightly. Cancellation of the work under the contract is an expensive and undesirable course of action. Generally, such terminations occur because of changes in Government requirements or because contract funding is not available.

The termination for convenience clause establishes the basis and measures of compensation that the contractor may recover as a consequence of termination. When a termination for convenience occurs, it results in extensive Government administrative actions involving accounting for property, determining contractor and subcontractor costs, and possibly paying termination settlement costs.

The obvious purpose of the termination for convenience clause is to permit the Government to halt performance under all or a portion of a contract even though the contractor is not in default. The clause also serves to provide an expeditious procedure for processing contractor's termination claims while relieving the Government from liability for breach of contract damages.

The contractor agrees that the Government has the right to terminate the contract, in whole or in part. In return, the Government agrees to pay the contractor its costs plus a reasonable profit on work done and preparations made on the terminated portion of the contract. The objectives of the termination for convenience clause are fairness, speed, and finality.

Steps Employed

The first step in termination for convenience is written notification to the contractor by the Contracting Officer. The notice clearly indicates that the contract is being terminated for the convenience of the Government. It also gives:

1. Effective date for the termination (usually the date of the notice)

2. The extent of the termination identifying what portion, if any, should be continued

3. Any special instructions

Upon receipt of the notice, the contractor is obligated to comply with the termination clause and the terms of the notice, that may include:

- Stopping work on terminated portions of the contract
- Terminating related subcontracts
- Continuing with un-terminated portions and promptly requesting any equitable adjustment in price on the continued portions
- Taking action to protect and preserve any Government property or to return it as directed by the Contracting Officer
- Settling claims and liabilities arising from terminated subcontracts
- Promptly submitting its own claim for settlement

Settlement Proposals

The Contracting Officer directs the actions of the contractor, reviews the settlement proposal, and promptly negotiates a settlement. A number of people, including the COR, may be involved in fulfilling these duties. One of the duties of the Contracting Officer in which the COR participates is in the settlement conference.

At the conference, the Contracting Officer will:

- Explain the general principles governing settlements under the relevant clause, including the contractor's obligations with respect to subcontracts
- Determine work status and clarify the extent of termination
- Determine the subcontracts being terminated and who is handling them for the contractor
- Make all arrangements for proper handling and disposition of Government property
- Discuss the form of the settlement proposal and accounting data required
- Establish a tentative negotiation settlement schedule

Settlement proposals submitted by contractors are subject to applicable cost principles (usually FAR Part 31), and the COR will generally be involved in evaluating their merit.

Termination for Convenience/Cause of Commercial Items

Government policy is that the Contracting Officer should exercise the Government's right to terminate a contract for commercial items either for convenience or for cause only when such a termination would be in the best interests of the Government. The Contracting Officer should consult with counsel prior to terminating for cause.

Termination for Cause

The paragraph in FAR 52.212-4 entitled "Excusable Delay" requires that contractors notify the Contracting Officer as soon as possible after commencement of any excusable delay. In most situations, this should eliminate the need for a show cause notice prior to terminating a contract. The Contracting Officer shall send a cure notice prior to terminating a contract for a reason other than late delivery.

The Government's rights after termination for cause shall include all the remedies available to any buyer in the marketplace. The Government's preferred remedy will be to acquire similar items from another contractor and to charge the defaulted contractor with any excess re-procurement costs together with any incidental or consequential damages incurred because of the termination.

When a termination for cause is appropriate, the Contracting Officer shall send the contractor a written notification regarding the termination. At a minimum, this notification shall:

1. Indicate the contract is terminated for cause
2. Specify the reasons for the termination
3. Indicate which remedies the Government intends to seek, or provide a date by which the Government will inform the contractor of the remedy
4. State that the notice constitutes a final decision of the Contracting Officer and that the contractor has the right to appeal under the disputes clause

Termination for the Government's Convenience

When the Contracting Officer terminates a contract for commercial items for the Government's convenience, the contractor shall be paid:

1. The percentage of the contract price reflecting the percentage of the work performed prior to the notice of the termination
2. Any charges the contractor can demonstrate directly resulted from the termination. The contractor may demonstrate such charges using its standard record keeping system and is not required to comply with cost accounting standards or the contract cost principles in part 31. The Government does not have any right to audit the contractor's records solely because of the termination for convenience.

Notes

Notes

Notes

Notes

Made in USA - Kendallville, IN
1026195_9781987529104
11.22.2019 1153